COME AND SEE THE SONGS OF STRANGE DAYS: POEMS ON FILMS

Fowler

ISBN:978-1-913642-38-9

Book designed by Aaron Kent

Edited by Aaron Kent

Broken Sleep Books (2021), Talgarreg, Wales

Contents

Come and See the Songs of Strange Days

SJ Fowler

‘It is a dark forest that people must go through, and they are scared to. But if they have a friend who says, ‘I know the forest’, they will happily follow.’

- *Lars Von Trier*

‘If you try to please audiences, uncritically accepting their tastes, it can only mean that you have no respect for them.’

- *Andrei Tarkovsky*

‘Words are but the shadows of actions.’

- *Democritus*

Songs from the Second Floor

First birth then chance,
mystery, death,
and a rare rabbit tablet poem is all.
A man weeping, realising
his son gone mad,
because he is a poet, of all things
we could be
walking like myself, as a dog,
imagined before-film towards
o the not working
the not the poet
being work
before the control implies
the eyes
seeing sad hues
as the son says,
Beloved be those
who drag the bodies of others into the street
Beloved be those
who seek not motivation,
who look not at themselves in mirrors,
and cameras, for
Beloved are the quenchable,
for they know not
when to stop
nor know what lives above
on the floor below.

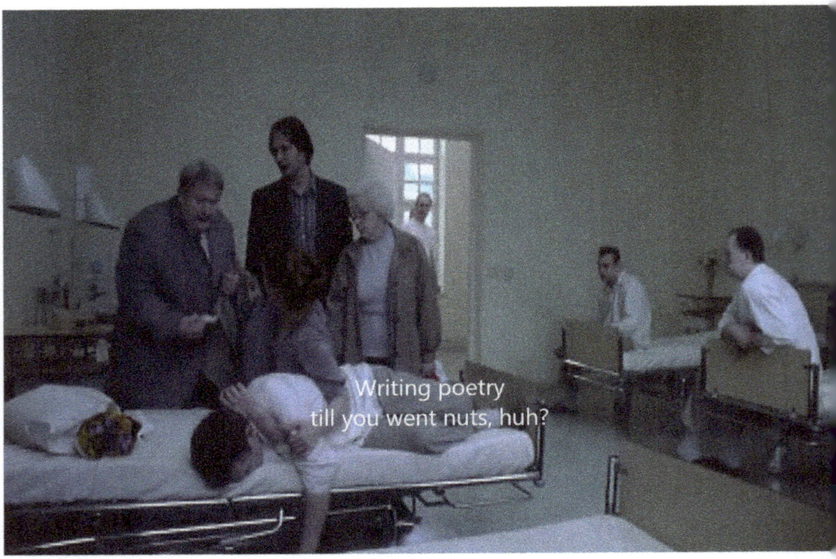
Writing poetry
till you went nuts, huh?

Yeah, he's lost his mind.
Writing poetry made him nuts.

RELEASE: 16 January 2001
DIRECTOR: Roy Andersson

L'enfant Sauvage

I was that ratboy from the forest
which was a big black mound of hair.
I haven't got a clue why.
I was the locked gate that will greet all children
the French basket, the noisy sock puppet.
The spectacular poems portraying spectacular beasts
in a paradise called revenge.
Who washes? Who would want to kiss mine jaw?
The overrated natural state of me,
is a little dog I loved that drowns in the sink.
This demonchest of the forest makes sense in savagery.
I want to bite everything and eat some of it.
I want your leg.
I want a nice tucked in curling ball and roll.
I want a cruel black dog tempting return.
I want to read, and then build about.
I want nice shops and promenades
and the fake smells of armpits.
I want the very process of perfumes from all over.
I want the liquid other bodies produce all over me in private.
I want to bring what I know from the darkness of the trees
into your lives.
Having learned more from the stupid, says Montaigne,
I now know less.

RELEASE: 26 February 1970
DIRECTOR: François Truffaut

November

The ladder of bread
leads to the roof
of slappy pigs.

↑

The sauna is full
of human sized chickens
birch thrashing
themselves.

↓

The dead are buried
treasure,
if you wait (long enough)
to dig them up.

→

Quite the surprise
to witness flagellation
as a permanent historical
host hog.

←

Wait for the woods in the dead
and you'll find
love lornly
walking
out.

RELEASE: 3 February 2017
DIRECTOR: Rainer Sarnet

Event Horizon

Go to the worst place you can imagine to encounter the best possible relief.

that place, that is belief, to imagine, your body can burst, in space.

Imagine it doing so. I'll guide you through, like a recent mediation.

It swells. all bits, every empty space. space. time in space. a bizarre bloating

why? no doctor knows. you can't imagine a *warhammer* version of hell

people used to imagine. everyday. but hell admits no scientific advice.

no airlock exists in medicine, nor science. no door to keep air in, if opened.

though hell is unlikely,   it is possible.

watch, repent. see a vision vision. a vision of chaos on the vista.

a horrible way to bring back the unimaginable

to punish ingrates. to force perspectives. to show hell off,

as though it were a child who teaches its parents.

imagine, watching, what might happen to people if hell is real.

what they, by an older measure, might deserve.

RELEASE: 15 August 1997
DIRECTOR: Paul WS Anderson

Mishima

Runaway Horses ("Asemic Poetry Written With A Splash Of Blood")

RELEASE: 15 May 1985
DIRECTOR: Paul Schrader

Julien Donkey-Boy

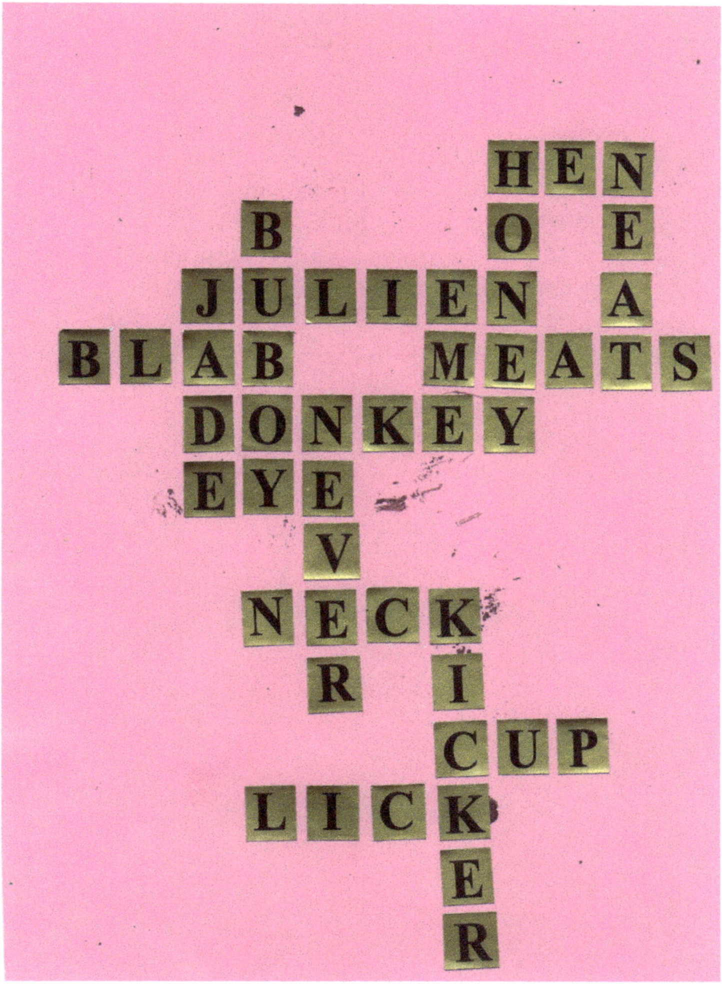
HEN
B O E
JULIEN A
BLAB MEATS
DONKEY
EYE
V
NECK
R I
CUP
LICK
E
R

RELEASE: 14 September 2000
DIRECTOR: Harmony Korine

Sicario

Con paz, con paz
Benicio sticks his finger deep into your ear.
To get information.
You give it.
Lo que necesitas.

Late to the orthodoxy, I receive the golden plug award.
I fix a leak, I touch the feathers. I bat my last.
The audience and parishioners boo, and refuse to suck
in their stomachs as I squeeze down the rows.

Later, Benicio says, affectionately, to me, quere mourir?

There is calamity and there is banality. There is language.
There is looking after other people's children.
There are terrible things, that I know, what they look like, Suelte la pistola

Pregunta paysano. quere mourir?

RELEASE: 29 June 2018
DIRECTOR: Denis Villeneuve

BAIT

CURSES BE EMMETTS
AS ANTHILLS

THE MUSIC PILCHARD'S LISTEN WHEN
THEY GRAB AND EAT THEIR TRAINERS
THAT SMELLS OF SOMETHING SEEN PINK,
FROM A HUT, TO THE SEA.

CORNISH IN THE NOT BORN PART OF YOU

THE GRAIN OF NOT WANTING TO LOOK
BOTH WAYS WHEN
CROSSING
ST KEVERNE ON THE LIZARD

LEAVING THE CITY,
WITHOUT BEING SEEN, TO BECOME THE COUNTRY
A REVERSE KESKERDH KERNOW
AN INVERTED MICHAEL AN GOF
FROM BLACKHEATH DOWN SOUTH
WEST

SOFT ROOTS
ARE CONNECTIONS BETWEEN
INCONTINENTS.
TAKING THE GET JET
SET, FROM THE DEEP
THE SEA OUR USELESS WAIT
ABOUT AGAIN IN VAIN
AFTER BEING INDIFFERENT TO THE
BEACH

BUT HOW LONG IS ARM'S LENGTH?
ABOUT BOTH
AND YOUR LEGS UP

AND THE MYTH;
WHERE THEY MEET, MATED
AND YOURS BORN,
THEN LOVED
THEN FORGOTTEN

A CORNISH
TURTLE EGO
A CORNISH MOLE HOLE
AS SOME SEE PRISON, A HEALTH
STATION TO STOP AT

A CHOUGH BREEDING WITH A
PILCHARD
LAYER OVER LAYER
NONE CAN PONDER
THE WOE TROUBLES
WHICH HAVE COME TO AFFLICT
THE CORNISH COUNCIL ESTATE
AND NONE DO TRY, BUT THIS, THAT
WHICH YOU'D PUT ON A HOOK TO
CATCH FISH

AN ORDINARY MAN BUT A MAN
WHOSE OWN LIFE HAD FATE

WHOSE BEST CURE IS PREVENTION...
BY DIVINE TEARS

SO THERE IS NO NEED TO BE UPSET
ONLY FRIENDS IN THE NIGHT
FISH THESE WATERS
MINE THESE ABANDONED HOLES IN
THE EARTH
AND REVENGE THE CAPITAL

IN THE UPPER CORNISH SEA
LIFE IS QUIET
IT IS
A WARM DRY VISIT

A DEVILS HORNS
A HAND INSIDE
A MORNING TIME I VISIT EYES CLOSED.

A DESERT CORNWALL
WELCOMES HOME IT'S SONS
REALLY READY THIS TIME TO MAKE THE
WORLD WORK.

RELEASE: 24 October 2019
DIRECTOR: Mark Jenkins

The 13th Warrior

A saying from the fireworm,
don't worry little brother, there are more.
Do men not wish to be bears?
Does the last man need not be a north man?
Do you listened? Do you learnt tongue?
Do you wash your face in a bowl of snot
I miss real friendship. I miss being held under covers.
It's cold in caves. It's cold in my jeans. It's cold,
for Ahmad ibn Fadlan, so he's writing everything down.
Do you round lamps of fire not grow into a worm?
Is there a cave? Switch then, to learn by watching,
switch, this is the message, and watch the spectacle of a monster
come to an end. Things become clear, the energy of the hunt has tired.
13 worries about the future of bears if cavemen wear them as costume.
13 worries about poems if they are only recited before death.
13 worries about the world if it is a massive impenetrable granite hole.
All told, the Vikings fall in love with an Arab, and Ahmad ibn Fadlan
falls in love too. He touches his chest and forehead in honour,
and asks what this honey alcohol is made of. In response, Buliwyf
is a good way to die, of which we'd all be relatively jealous.

RELEASE: 27 August 1999
DIRECTOR: John McTiernan

Gorillas in the Mist

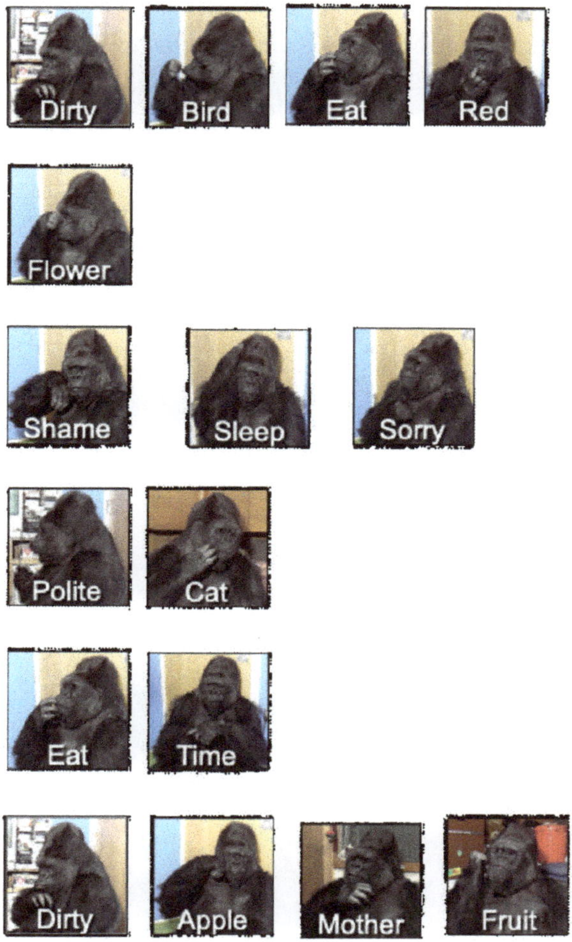
Dirty
Bird
Eat
Red
Flower
Shame
Sleep
Sorry
Polite
Cat
Eat
Time
Dirty
Apple
Mother
Fruit

RELEASE: 23 September 1988
DIRECTOR: Michael Apted

Last of the Mohicans

Magua couldn't give two shits until he has both of his arms horribly broken. A gun stock warclub, swung down by Chingachgook, has smashed his shoulder. He shows no sign of pain.

You will remember this moment. After the music, after Russell Means' forward roll. Magua and Chingachook holding the moment, staring eye to eye. They seem to contemplate the existential catastrophe which is befalling them.

Running, at a set pace, through woods, holding a rifle, the son of C. Day Lewis. You will remember the inexorable quality of these scenes, the romance that makes experience of inevitability. The frontier as the only land available to the poorer Europeans, where the colonials disappear into the trees, off screen.

There is romantic murder to follow. The terrible features of the war out there in the Americas.

Hawkeye looks up, and tells Cora, that at the birth of its suns, its mother will die.

She has a vision of a view from the trees, into a valley of death.

Under a knife.

Instead, the gunstock warclub as a symbol of something historical, cultural and technical. A symbol of absorption, necessity. A rushing up, or rather down, of awful record.

Magua wishes to start a corporation with the crown negotiating service. He seems to understand fully that British policy is to make the world England. He is ready to adapt. The murder of his family seems to have provided motive.

Magua is temporarily French. He hears the British say the French haven't the nature for war, and he takes notes, mentally. The British officer laziness means they'd rather eat and make love with their faces than fight.

Magua will need to love often towards new death to start his revision. But there is often that anyway. Often as in always. Magua was Huron, captured by Mohawk, fighting Mohican. Wes Studi is Cherokee. Magua understand English very well. Magua, tomahawk in hand, yellow and back shawl, black collar.

Cora's vision. Her father, dying. Her sister, dying. The children of the two face, under the knife. And so it happens. An ambush in the valley, the trees alive. Cora asking to rest, knifeless. Instead, the ball-headed warclub as a symbol of something. Armourlessness. Ingenuity. Pitched battles. Formation fighting versus guerrilla warfare. The battle versus the war.

Magua's has been broken down, fractured, scattered and misunderstood. That's to be expected, given the context. The war in the Americas, how it begins, the flavour of that. The lasting effects. And the coming of those who bring night with them.

You will not
remember, we cannot
escape what we
are by using the
word why, or who.

Magua holds knife
and tomahawk,
they are above him.

He kills Uncas.

Previously, to stay
alive, Duncan
sacrifices his life for
Cora.

Then Magua kills
Uncas. Alice leaps
from a rock after
Uncas has slid down it.

These are the love
stories worth telling.

Magua eats no less than whites. Tomahawks reddening. Magua would have back more land than they'd use. Magua would use the way of the night. When questioned by Hawkeye, he looks back at him as though it is a stupid question.

Chingachgook drives the gunstock war club through the gut and liver of Magua. The camera waits for his face to fall as you remember the scene with Cora's father, and the realisation of her vision.

Magua has stood and holds in his right hand a human heart.

RELEASE: 25 September 1992
DIRECTOR: Michael Mann

Benny's Video

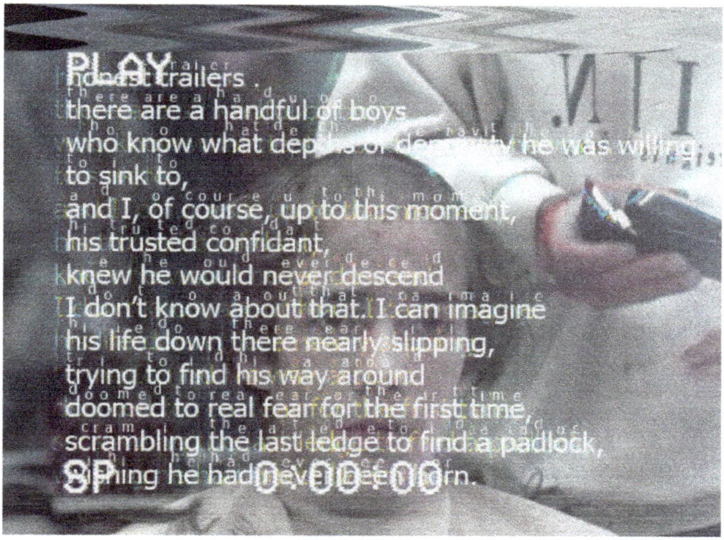
PLAY
honest trailers .
there are a handful of boys
who know what dep he was willing
to sink to,
and I, of course, up to this moment,
his trusted confidant,
knew he would never descend
I don't know about that. I can imagine
his life down there nearly slipping,
trying to find his way around
doomed to real fear for the first time,
scrambling the last ledge to find a padlock,
ing he had rn.
SP 0:00:00

RELEASE: 4 March 1993
DIRECTOR: Michael Haneke

Dogtooth

as is often said, incisors /
competition / incest

parented with a glass knife =
water babies

the body's bitter medicine
that forgets

how often you leave, that's how
important it is to run

a film better on endless
repeats, to white haired

little childs with little
antlers and the soft egg flower
show

plucking petals like a
schoolgirl, housecats killing
your kin

stooped over like a hunch - hard
to love, hard to leave

a warning telephone
translation from the Greek,
where

if they'd been gentle, then
they wouldn't have been us(e)

RELEASE : 11 March 2010
DIRECTOR: Jorgos Lanthimos

True Romance

Gg Gg Gg Gg Gg
AaAaA aA Aa AaA
ssssSSssSS SssS SSssSSssss
ee ee EE ee ee
Nn nn nn nn nN
H h H h H
aa au au aa aaaa au au aa aa
u uu uu uu uu UU uu uu uu uu uYYu uu uu uu uu UU uu uu uu uu u
Ee ee eEE ee eE
rrrr r r r r R R r r r r rrrr

A sound poem to be performed to the melody of Carl Orff's Gassenhauer (a song featured in True Romance, as well as in films such as Badlands (1973), Ratcatcher (1999), Finding Forrester (2000), Monster (2003), Michael Moore's Capitalism: A Love Story (2009))

RELEASE : 15 October 1993
DIRECTOR: Tony Scott

Badlands

Belonging in the forest

in the spider tr**A**p of the murder / in the best light of young use America
the hour of mur**D**erers is an act of love as naive as a field trip

Love is
on **A** road
it belo**N**gs to
the light of day, to ca**D**illacs on the
great plain**S**

RELEASE : 15 October 1973
DIRECTOR: Terence Malick

Blade Runner

▲ sister texts us its our mother's
birthd▲y
has she resurrected? wonder

We understand now. ▲n ▲ndroid.
Wh▲t ▲ failed eye test c▲n le▲d to.
Good t▲ste, b▲d vision.

▲sk wh▲t h▲s been repl▲ced ▲nd design
eyes to le▲k.

Ch▲rco▲l synthesis over neon lips.
Robot sn▲kes e▲ting b▲tteries.

Envying the tempor▲ry, whose memories
didn't definitely.

RELEASE : 25 June 1982
DIRECTOR: Ridley Scott

Little Otik

RELEASE : 25 January 2001
DIRECTOR: Jan Švankmajer

Dau

with Maria Malinovskaya

Q - The DAU that can be told is not the eternal DAU, not the first cinematic project about isolation. Was it filmed for people in isolation?
A - Not solely so. For if it sounds familiar, it's not a film only wishing. Not physically so, rather than psychologically self-so.

Q - Are cinemas still popular in Russia? A Stalinist show, would you participate?
A - Only if the cast was small, and they inevitably asked for me by name.

Q - The biopic of a Soviet scientist Lev Landau, what do you know about him?
A - Nothing until the temporary Dau.

Q - Why do people remember the Union?
A - the mouse utopia inside any system, any society, any family, any single mind attempting to escape into poetry and not attempting to escape into poetry, poetry attempting to escape into life

Q - Have you ever written any documentary poetry ?
A - I steal in my own words, barely, like wrapping food inside another food, like not reporting on my neighbours. I document that which can't be said directly, or shouldn't be. I learned from Russian poets that being unable to speak plainly is best. I document for myself my not saying what is obvious to me.

Q - Are we informants who don't know that they are informants or are we the way we are because we see others informing?
A - To have a chance to play with petty revenge and tell their stories to me because they love me, because they want to be with me, because they need somebody to talk to except the voices in their heads who agree to become just characters if it is the only opportunity to be.

Q - Would you agree? Is our Dau answering honestly?
A –

Q - Why is Dau? An old world? The impermanent world, the easiest thing to say?
A – Nostalgia as the enemy of amnesia.

Q - Who are the Russian actors?
A - famous scientists notorious criminals musicians artists skins former KGB officers porn-actresses. No poets, you see?

RELEASE: 24 January 2019
DIRECTOR: Ilya Khrzhanovsky

Man Bites Dog

Come with me and I'll show you what you've done.

I wander off from the cameras and imagine yourself in a field I can see in the distance.
The details don't matter too much.
You're walking. You come across a body.
You were talking, I interrupted. You were speaking of the *craft* of murder, the failings of architecture, your own poetry and your classical music, which you play with your girlfriend.

'Oh no,' you think, suddenly, 'what if they think I killed them?'

This would be a reasonable thought to have, sooner or later, after discovery.
But better not said, *out loud*. So many questions would follow.

The investigation would necessarily seek out information not only about the body you've discovered, but all the information that surrounds it.
Like zooming out of google maps.
You'd soon be inculcated. That is, *informed.*

We begin with the details of the corpse.
It's eyes, eyelashes, hairline.
Then indents around the eyes, from glasses?
The clothes.
What is under its fingernails? What is that earthy smell?
A first time for everything.

The field.
The surroundings.
The nearby road, town, city, county, region, country, continent.
Can you navigate without a map?
What if you lose your way?
What if you need to return to this field, to the place of burial.
What were you doing in that field?

The body would not be useful alone.
It is true, the body begins
but without the body there is nothing to worry about, absolutely.

You wonder why you just left it out.

Without other people worrying about everything that surrounds the body, in tandem, in a matrix, in a constellation, then they'll never be able to prove your innocence.
You realise, there is no single body in the field.

The field is full of bodies.
Of all different hues.
All at different depths. All kinds of time. Degradation in stages.
Is hue the problem?
A lack of it.

Or something deeper, more ambiguous, more threatening, than shade?
Than decomposition.
Something more important, but harder to understand, and so easier to ignore, in favour of just *look*.

The field must be cultivated with the utmost of care,
if we are to find the killer,
for its agency is disappeared by the generosity of knowledge.

Someone has told you the conditions.
Don't kill. Definitely don't kill for fun.
That is purposeless and murder.

What is given and accepted will rapidly become
the appearance of being *found*,
with all the pretence of being essential,
though it is simply that which has been discovered by someone else.
It plasters over that knowledge which you make for yourself
that what might have a stronger claim on an inner truth.
You are alive, and they are not.
The very act of discovery itself.

The more time you spend in the field, the more you are inherited, fed and interjected, the more proselytising your feeling about it is.
There's an irony here, though.
For you did kill the corpse, It Happened Near Your Home.

You were reacting, self-defence or not, you were trying to impress, to describe, to show off, you were being filmed.
But the dead are still dead, and you killed them.
Whatever they said. Whatever they did.
I mean, you might as well become more involved in the murders?
First as accomplice but eventually taking an active role.
It's not boring at least. It's meaningful, in a way.
It's a kind of occupational hazard, for a crew member, such as you.

RELEASE : 1992
DIRECTORS: Benoît Poelvoorde, Rémy Belvaux, André Bonzel

Big Wednesday

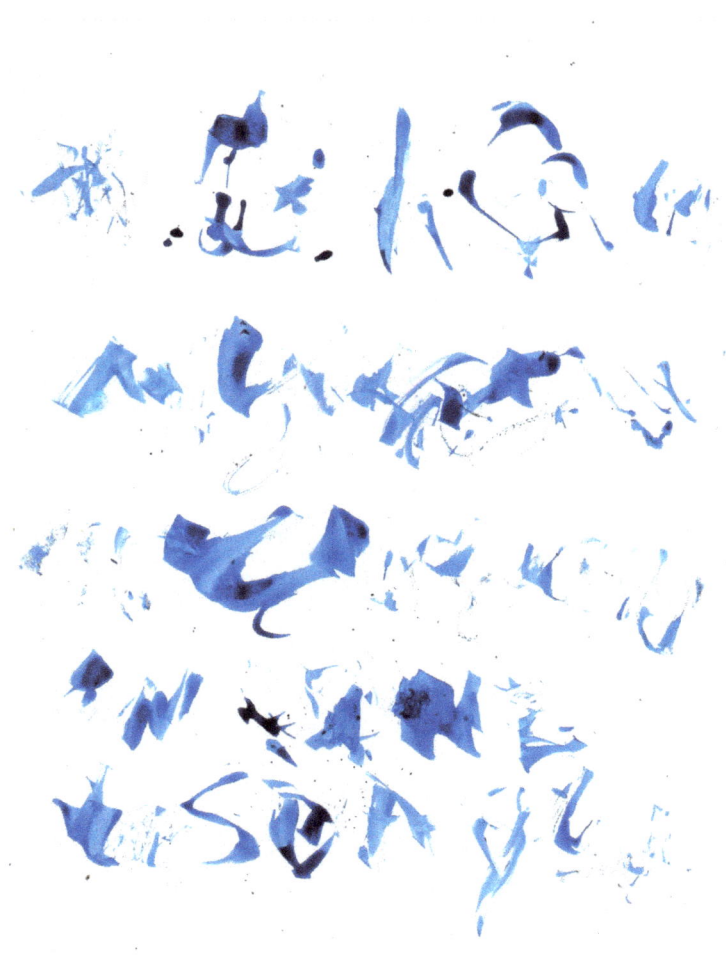

RELEASE: 7 August 1980
DIRECTOR: John Milius

Sátántangó

what every tree [The News Is They Are Coming]
gushes over books that havent been read. [We Are Resurrected]
things to be finished. [Knowing Something]
the abeyance of time. [The Job of the Spider]
an apocalyptic sense of crisis [Unraveling]
repeat the name. village, run-down. [The Devil's Tit, Satan's Tango]
mysterious criminal or prophet comes along. [Irimiás Gives A Speech]
gets them all to move to another village. [The Perspective From the Front]
we don't know why. [Going to Heaven? Having Nightmares?]
('Heaven is sad') [The Perspective From The Rear]
Destruction and Sorrow Beneath the Heavens is sadder. [Just Trouble and Work]
a long mirror. [The Circle Closes]

RELEASE: 22 December 1994
DIRECTOR: Bela Tarr

Ossuary

MORIENS

RELEASE : 1970
DIRECTOR: Jan Švankmajer

This Filthy Earth

there's none could cure you
of your ignorance
I mean that's great
we love you as you are
Anselm Hollo

To have a good soil that produces face is a reet
where surroundings are with a fat accents
and physical gestures of unlikely drinks marriage.

A fat to wish earth well, in lay of people, an
never have stomach upsets, and recognise nowt
the choice in constant farm behaviour.

Life half, and boring out of fear and fright
or make a light mystery
so clowt as to create

hurt about and feel full tank
instead of nowt
or stopped, or bog, or lob, or
weaks stomachs pecking the claim.

RELEASE: 2 November 2001
DIRECTOR: Andrew Kötting

Irreversible

Myet,s ʇɥə bnɹɔʞəsʇ ʍɐʎ ʇo sɐqoʇɐƃə ʍɥɐʇ ʍonlpu,ʇ qə səəu¿
Oɹ sɥonlpu,ʇ qə¿
Sɥoʍ ʇɥə əup ɟɹɹsʇ˙
ɹɹıƃɥʇəu ʎonɹ ɟɹıəup˙
Holp ɔɐɯəɹɐ ou ɹəʌnlsıou˙
Hɐʌə uo ɐ qəəʇɥoʌəu pəɐɟuəss˙
Suɐd ɐɹɯs ʍıʇɥ ɐ ʞuəə ɐqoʌə ʇɥə əlqoʍ˙
Myɐʇ,s ləss doʍəɹɟnl ʇɥɐu loʌə¿
∀ pəlnsıou' ıu ɹəʌəɹsə˙
∀ ɥɐlɟ lıʇəɹ oɟ soɐd
ıu ɐ ɥnɯɐu sızəp qɐƃ˙
∀ ɔɐɹɹoʇ pɐuƃlıuƃ˙
∀u nudləɐsɐuʇ ɹnɯonɹ˙
∀u nuɹəɔoʌəɹɐqlə uıƃɥʇɯɐɹə˙
∀ qıʇʇəɹ ɥəɐɹʇ˙
∀ qnɹuıuƃ ɯɐsʞ˙
∀ ʇəɹɹıqlə ɟɐʇə oɟ ɟıɹə˙
∀ ƃɹıəɟ onʇ oɟ ɐ ɯıup˙
I,ll ƃəʇ ʎon ıu ʇɥə əup˙
⊥ɥə ɐusʍəɹ ɐʇ ʇɥə qəƃıuuıuƃ˙
⊥ɥə əxʇıuƃnısɥəɹ sɐʎs ʎon ʍonlpu,ʇ ʞuoʍ ɯə ıɟ ʎon sɐʍ ɯə˙
⊥ɥə ɹɐdə ɐusʍəɹs˙

RELEASE: 1 August 2002
DIRECTOR: Gaspar Noé

Congo

> Munro was conscious of the deteriorating situation with both Elliott and Ross. He had seen it happen on expeditions before, particularly when scientists and technical people were involved. Scientists worked all day in laboratories where conditions could be rigorously regulated and monitored. Sooner or later, scientists came to believe that the outside world was just as controllable as their laboratories. Even though they knew better, the shock of discovering that the natural world followed its own rules and was indifferent to them represented a harsh psychic blow.
>
> Michael Crichton

You think an eye for an eye is Amy talking *gorilla*
but remember the eyeball. Remember the Lost City.
Linger on the word Zinj.
Amy the talking gorilla, smokes, drinks and knows who is lying.
Amy sees we live to settle scores.
That you're in better hands than you should be.
Amy hears, *whose Kafka, tell me*? Amy knows you have a big mouth
and every human shows her that.
Amy, smells you have a paper bag full of cash, stapled shut,
you have a one way ticket to Solomon's Mines
From Amy, to lasers, to the cry of timing, to the talking volcano,
Amy is a gorilla in the camp, signing. But that isn't enough.
Amy is technology, the invention of resources.
Amy is a jewel in a gun, making extinction swift.
Amy is on billboards being celebrity status.
Amy is in before coffee became expensive, like diamonds.
Amy is the headline you no longer even deign to believe.
She is the coin you will order on the phone and never spend.
She is the stamp of unsaid approval from staying silent.
She is the art gallery where you read the labels and see no pictures.
She is Pablo Neruda and Cesar Vallejo. She is everyone who ignores me.
Amy is unquenchable, translatable, caring and sane.
She exists to save Peter, and we are he.

Jungle here.
Jungle is.

Jungle here.
Jungle is.
Jungle place
here

Amy see
jungle here.

No.

Amy is poet gorilla
Amy live
Amy house.
Amy want
cigarette.

They worried.
They worried
men
worry they
worried
problems.

man lie
Peter
ground hurt
we come
bad place
People die here

Things come.
Bad things
come things
come bad
Bad things.

People bad.
No believe
people
bad
things
come
Amy
no
go
No go
Amy
P
F
POSTAGE
REVENUE
3p

Bad place old
place no go
Amy good
gorilla
Bad place old
place no go

RELEASE: 9 June 1995
DIRECTOR: Frank Marshall

Ivul

The situation of the child was an impossible one.
Ernest Becker

terrain relations sneaky secret
the egg wants to be a bird and cracks
by our own reasoning
by our I mean *the family* we mustve
done something terrible to deserve
the punishment visited upon us
and by punishment I mean *erotic*
I mean throwing sheeps from cliffs after mort
I mean leaving Russia
I mean the bulge of white pants on a girl
I mean I agree
I mean cut down the tree, burned it up
and I watched a man is made by ghosty planting
and then goes on and on and
I agree it does seem best
to never stand upon the earth again
a gentle hand to guide me down

RELEASE: 20 January 2010
DIRECTOR: Andrew Kötting

A Dangerous Method

We see that the poet embodies the double function of the ego ideal. Seen from the outside, the poet creates a new personal ideal for the masses, a creation to which he was driven by his inner conflicts arising from the formation of his own ideal. Dissatisfied with the ideal of the group, he forms his own individual ideal in order to proffer it to the group, without whose recognition his creation remains very unsatisfactory. ⊠ The pressure that the poet feels to solicit recognition of his new ideal from the group reveals that he created it not only to satisfy his own narcissism, but also to replace the old common ideal with a new one. ⊠ The tragedy of every great poetic personality is that when this aim succeeds, it must finally lead to disappointment instead of satisfaction, just as the primal deed does. The reason is that as his personal ideal is generally recognised and appreciated, it becomes established as another group ideal, the very thing that he wishes to shun.

Otto Rank - Don Juan Legend, 1924

The poet who had ⊠ set himself free from the group in his imagination, is nevertheless able (as Rank has further observed) to find his way back to it in reality. For he goes and relates to the group his hero's deeds, which he has invented. At bottom this hero is no one but himself. Thus he lowers himself to the level of reality, and raises his hearers to the level of imagination.

Sigmund Freud - Group Psychology

RELEASE: 10 February 2012
DIRECTOR: David Cronenberg

Conan the Barbarian

> "Of all evil I deem you capable: Therefore I want good from you. Verily, I have often laughed at the weaklings who thought themselves good because they had no claws."
>
> Friedrich Nietzsche

Conan waits until the vulture begins to eat him to eat the vulture. There is a potent metaphor here for how I feel about how others feel. Conan is littered with symbols.

Metaphor upon metaphor until the words become a wash rippling muscles and a declaration of what is good in life. Not everyone has an answer to that question.

The similarity of cults is remarkable. A chronicle of killing hippies. Milius and Oliver Stone sat in a dark room, laughing, smoking. They write, *Known is his god, he lives in the earth, he shakes with rage. Conan then forgets the secret.*

They go on. *No one in this world can you trust. Not men, not women, not beasts. This. This you can trust.* They scribble. *The village raid as most of human history. No one would know his people had ever lived at all.*

What is best in life? Conan is written. His hands and face are poems and he comes back to life, from death, having died upon the tree of woe.

A few years ago Set was just another snake cult. It is said they are deceivers. Milius reflecting upon a creeping liberation movement. The riddle of steel is that flesh is stronger. But metaphorically. As literally, it is not.

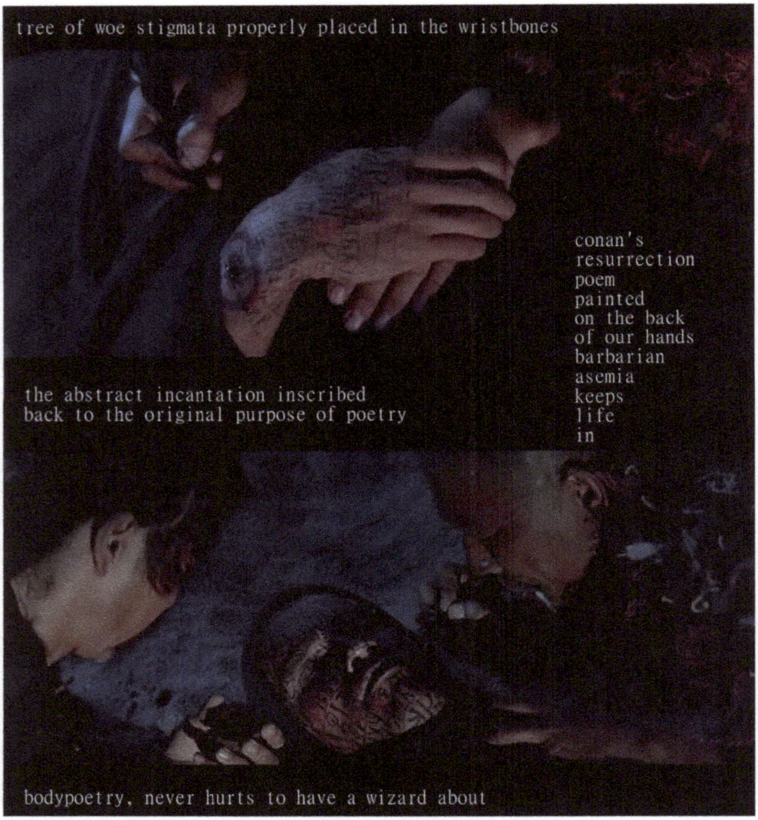
tree of woe stigmata properly placed in the wristbones
conan's
resurrection
poem
painted
on the back
of our hands
barbarian
asemia
keeps
life
in
the abstract incantation inscribed
back to the original purpose of poetry
bodypoetry, never hurts to have a wizard about

RELEASE: 2 April 1982
DIRECTOR: John Milius

Pierrepoint

The job of the most closely guarded secrets,
there is no sense to prolonging the agony.

Those who have paid the price are innocent now,
or so says the man who attempts leaves himself beyond the
noose.

Something beneath feet, disappears. A lever, a switch.
A suggestion that one follows me.

Fairness isn't weakness, for if one wishes swiftly,
that should be granted. It's mercy.

The world should know our executions were the most efficient and
humane.
Without shot, or strangling. With the separation of vertebrae.

The time for a brew that must be denied, for who wants to fall
behind?
The leaner the man, the shorter the drop.

RELEASE: 12 September 2005
DIRECTOR: Adrian Shergold

The Vikings

Viking   tourist.
Europe tour   980
a letter that   makes a king in
the time of soft   climes
in the age of   soft people are
bound to dig
& is re-   markably how
many will state
of your fave   directly when
you are at it in   the chair
oaf lover   I'm not sorry
off this kind
but   that is a kind of
exception   that sent me
to writing?   Iced?
Overseas ill
for the thread   of King
Y   day comets
that competed   comforts
that is an   alphabet reliant
on a tree
rather than the   conduit itself
I was present
I was   a wrist tour
a wittily sight   a girl
on the bed for   he

meeting out   on the watery
that was far
assured   fair beauty
funny set
Viking tissue. Worrier
Viking risotto
Coming rosier
Europe tot
do you take me
for a serf? Whom
you control with
your code?
there is no labour
that is honourable
only in not laboring is
there live love
in feeding others whom bear
better feed   themselves
but what had   that to do with
work?
work is   horror idiot
need of being   busy. I'm never
busy.
until I had to   leave a mes-
sage
& so the   gecko letter
came into the   sky

the Gway   way unleashed
beyond human   control
no see   the double is
after the bomb
north-   ern Writing and
rissian food
down the   bluewater
that's the pretty   river
filled with   pretty water
moving beyond   this letter
to the next one   (if you keep
saying yes I am   going
to break   your nouse)
what is up? a   spout
burnt up   aren't here, but
spidery whiles,   upside down
draining hole   occurring, we
don't need you
but we will   take you

Olaf,
you went
down? You, once I
was a folk doctor
+ I saw a monkey ride a
mottorship
he hit a corner
at 90 knots
& his heart
came out of his chest

I love North but wait
until you're auld (45)
it will undoubtedly ma-
jestic   it into his
report that the
plastic tub, like a natu-
ıl geyser, seems to

ccasional erup-
;
ɔy bear

ı a boy

ɟ bear boys

ɟ; project descrip-
ɔn   tour 6-6—6 En-
emies
Killer swords, swords
with bent, or pulled up
blades
are found in burials ex-
cavated from bogs,
lakes, rivers
the deliberate
destruction of such
highly valued objects
puts them beyond
the use of the living
after all
the living is dead
then   interwo-
ven

with
sword
deterring grave
robbers
while the sound of the
jaw   you describeus as
princes rather than kings
but they aren't used to
actual push as much as
the same ways
as kings else-
where in the Europe
oh I am Eirik that mighty
letter,
the might of being a
maker of men
rued the land from
beneath his helmet of
terror
in York the K
reigned rigig o
over rainy s
but,
say t
the w
brother
message c
arund   Me
golden one
o the two lands (whic
are nothing to the full
number of Hives)
who foresees this many
books being written?
only for their chil-
dren though
what possible better use
for the human potential
in discovering a new
people
of the coun-
try than
physical power & natural
fitness like an inspired
Viking?

RELEASE: 28 June 1958
DIRECTOR: Richard Fleischer

The Relic

The tasty hypothalamus
that is carried within the human
museum that leads dogs
into tunnels
from sea to land.

Rising above the designation
monster,
the stranger has transformed.
Whitney walks into the dark room
of his old job,
where two things
sit at a table and talk of travel.
It joins the conversation,
saying 'I have also travelled'
and people listen
for he has changed.

The body of us wasted
for a small speck of brain.
like the film with more
than it should be.
The nights of a museum,
without taboo,
giving memory to
beasts.

RELEASE: 10 January 1997
DIRECTOR: Peter Hyams

The Ghost and the Darkness

We will not complain.
We will not change our protagonists.
We will have to admit, it is a serious problem.
There is not a healthy one thing to look up into.
There is not any cache in being,
but there is some in being consumed.
The animals come to relieve us,
and to kill for pleasure in parody.
In a normal lions it is feeding that is working,
but all this, under trees,
We waited watching.
We caused litigation among former neighbours.
Cats are inevitably unknown, fantastic.
The whole territory was eighteen ninety eight.
They should make up. But they won't.
Along lines of communication to Tsavo,
from posts, boring the train,
with visions of a wife and child murdered,
by creature, under cold sheets, we listen. we love it here.
Hoping yet not hoping the rifle is adequate, untested
and in the late morning, startled to the sound of roaring,
we said 'you're going to regret doing that',
and began to smell the smell of Bernard's blood.
In a sink. On the white sheets. In the thickets of thorns.

RELEASE: 12 June 1997
DIRECTOR: Stephen Hopkins

Budbringeren (Junk Mail)

when Christiania was a dump
when it had faces, expressions, delivered
ways of steaming open an envelope
in a kind kind of eventual benevolent absorption
I watched on, surprised

not making the best of what it had
the city held unsolid depictions of the poor, cold
workers being rude.
though at least not that outwardly sad.

they murmur Postman Pat, Postman Pat
Postman Pat and his black and white cat
early in the morning, just as day is dawning,

Christiania becomes Oslo, becomes developed
voices change, accents. even languages.
still, your letters won't arrive
because you need someone to deliver them

RELEASE: 16 July 1998
DIRECTOR: Pål Sletaune

Margin Call

a lie to talk of a demarcation
a fraction of the legal / illegal economy
and a lie that the money class are against
for where does the money rest?
my portland road, my london banker
here is the new brand
violence as friendly, as a soldier on the street

you are my employee
i reserve the right to punish you

for your monoply of decision
i have a bird shaped osmosis
of chemical hierarchy

& the distinctly Crusader influence in the attitude to travel
storming walls
a bistro full of smoke sobbing into a cigar I hope

limited stocks
only for the people who read

a French maid's uniform

a mattress made of what is dead

commanding an army of Midoclorian

so don't underestimate the word style
is an estimable word, where i come from
it is too late for deals

while I have invested my money with zeal
into farms

big guns, fancy
are you scared at this part? you want to get out of here?

vain is the thing that does not heal suffering in man
for there is nothing new happening in the universe,

the invasions of Britain
really began a culture of invasions
which had ramifications

helped us understand we are a colony

endless screaming decapitations

RELEASE: 10 November 2011
DIRECTOR: JC Chandor

Black Moon

[illegible] unicorn

RELEASE: 1975
DIRECTOR: Louis Malle

You, the Living

So muchismade of delusion
but manismans delight
like singeing talk
like brass music
like not negative nature
not nothing without ceremony
not nurture yielding elegies
not a nice new
electric chair neither
o but definitely
familiar forms of ludic
emerge from nature
asananti dote
presenting after collecting
small lessmaller incidents
like pulling a dog to
o bobbo who likes you to
o nobody understands you to
o what lies beneath the tablecloth trick?
secrets
without secrets
nothing can berevealed
notatesta ment inparts
like tiny crashes
like cornflakes living
through glued guts
stuffed back into screens
that whisper hisses
you areplayingverywell
that&salliwantedatosay

I didn't understand why,
but I got the feeling it was my fault...

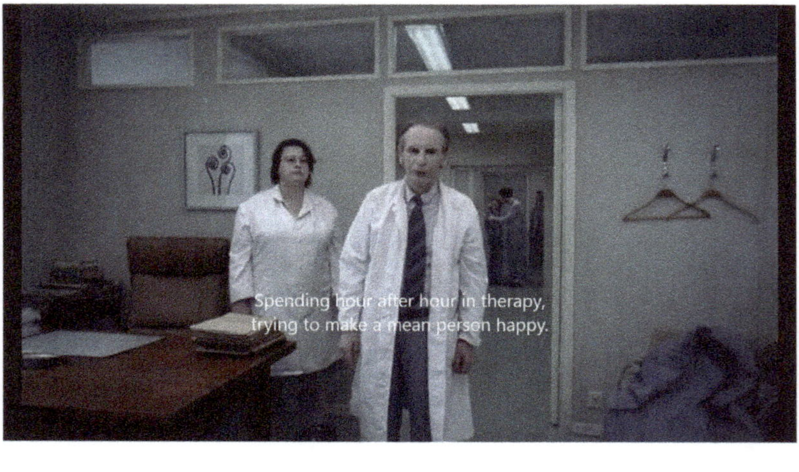
Spending hour after hour in therapy,
trying to make a mean person happy.

RELEASE: 21 September 2007
DIRECTOR: Roy Andersson

Ordet

> Since boredom advances and boredom is the root of all evil,
> no wonder, then, that the world goes backwards.
> Kierkegaard

No rest the wicked
who love secretly,
who go mad, Johannes,
who wander into miracles
to feel fortune as uncertain knowing.
The miracle is an island where matter evaporates.
Where there are only hard coffins,
and leaking wood.
This is a Danish kind of prison,
to believe, faithfully.
A kind of post-miracle past.
An unkind passing of possibility.
An unfair request of the dead,
to make them living.
Inevitably, hand twitching,
we hope it is not us who comes back to life.

RELEASE: 10 January 1955
DIRECTOR: Carl Theodor Dreyer

Tender Mercies

winds don'**T**
throw ston**E**s at
    meals a**N**d
        two **D**ollars i too
            hav**E** not seen.
            The**R**e's only so much happiness to trust, only so

            Much
            r**E**ality that
        hu**R**ts.
    But su**C**h music.
In it the real**I**ty that
            g**E**ts out beside
    your **S**ystem.

RELEASE: 8 September 1983
DIRECTOR: Bruce Beresford

Bells from the Deep

> I wanted to get shots of pilgrims crawling around on the ice trying to catch a glimpse of the lost city, but as there were no pilgrims around I hired two drunks from the next town and put them on the ice. One of them has his face right on the ice and looks like he is in very deep meditation. The accountant's truth: he was completely drunk and fell asleep, and we had to wake him at the end of the take.
>
> Werner Herzog

A Jesus, I heard about.
I was running with him, meekly.
Stumbling across the world's great farm
and the releasing of the royal cows.
In their midst the cow whom Sonja
of metal teeth called evil,
flames from snout and anus,
bully, beefy, foreign, unfairly declaimed.

Then taking a phone in hand when asked
to kneel upon a sacred hill, there was, cattle aside,
an exchange of illness. Exhaustion, genital burning,
hypertension. The unnameable
sickness in between.

But let us remember, probably dead now
Yuri Yurevitch Yurieff, an orphaned bell ringer.
Timeless, non-linear love
in the poor man's beauty.

RELEASE: 7 September 1993
DIRECTOR: Werner Herzog

The Burden of Dreams

I don't want to live in
a world where there is
no lions anymore. Nor a
world where there are
no people like lions.
And there are no people
like lions. And there
people are like lions.
Werner Herzog
2000 miles to walk free of the jungle this way.
1500 this way, 1500 the other way.
And finally, 500 miles out.
This is the point of synchronicity.
The lair of the white turkey in the rainforest.
German rubber, feral pig. Turtle arrows.
Where mud swallows ghosts who report back from death
that, in the end, all are accused of making it hard on
themselves.

RELEASE: 1 October 1982
DIRECTOR: Les Blank

Meine Liebste Freunde (My Best Fiend)

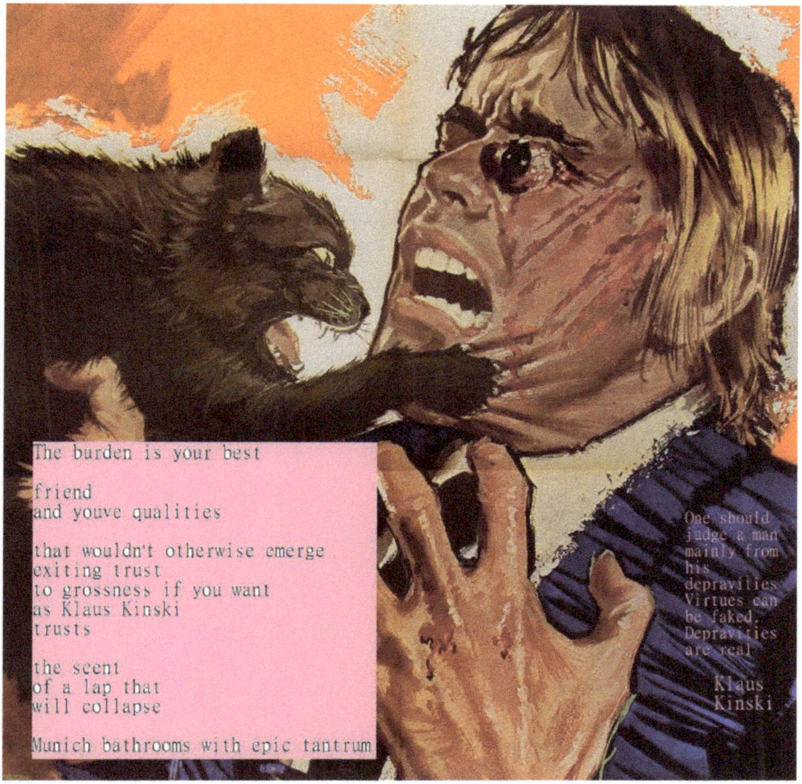
The burden is your best

friend
and youve qualities

that wouldn't otherwise emerge
exiting trust
to grossness if you want
as Klaus Kinski
trusts

the scent
of a lap that
will collapse

Munich bathrooms with epic tantrum

One should
judge a man
mainly from
his
depravities
Virtues can
be faked.
Depravities
are real

Klaus
Kinski

RELEASE: 7 October 1999
DIRECTOR: Werner Herzog

Heftig og begeistret (Cool and Crazy)

Once morose, always morose.
The troll who won't dance
will have his tail tied in his pants.

It is amazing what an old drug addict is capable of.
What rules like everywhere else,
as it has always been.

A multi-instrumentalist, just not good at any of them.
An old choir in chaos in the cold.
Some need to steal, some burn down houses.
Others need neatly in the snow.

For he who is lazy will soon go crazy.
The old have anchored,
being satyrs in their youth.

Being cased in thick skinn,
they say the men of Berlevåg
have to be shot, for they will not die.

RELEASE: 8 February 2002
DIRECTOR: Knut Erik Jensen

Groundhog Day

then put your little hand in mine there ain't no hill or mountain we can't climb babe I got
you babe I got you babe ok campers rise and shine and don't forget your booties because
it's cold out there today its cold out there everyday what is this miami beach? not hardly
then put your little hand in mine there ain't no hill or mountain we can't climb babe I got
you babe I got you babe ok campers rise and shine and don't forget your booties because
it's cold out there today its cold out there everyday what is this miami beach? not
then put your little hand in mine there ain't no hill or mountain we can't climb babe I got
you babe I got you babe ok campers rise and shine and don't forget your booties because
it's cold out there today its cold out there everyday what is this miami beach?
then put your little hand in mine there ain't no hill or mountain we can't climb babe I got
you babe I got you babe ok campers rise and shine and don't forget your booties because
it's cold out there today its cold out there everyday what is this Miami
then put your little hand in mine there ain't no hill or mountain we can't climb babe I got
you babe I got you babe ok campers rise and shine and don't forget your booties because
it's cold out there today its cold out there everyday what is this
then put your little hand in mine there ain't no hill or mountain we can't climb babe I got
you babe I got you babe ok campers rise and shine and don't forget your booties because
it's cold out there today its cold out there everyday what is
then put your little hand in mine there ain't no hill or mountain we can't climb babe I got
you babe I got you babe ok campers rise and shine and don't forget your booties because
it's cold out there today its cold out there everyday what
then put your little hand in mine there ain't no hill or mountain we can't climb babe I got
you babe I got you babe ok campers rise and shine and don't forget your booties because
it's cold out there today its cold out there everyday
then put your little hand in mine there ain't no hill or mountain we can't climb babe I got
you babe I got you babe ok campers rise and shine and don't forget your booties because
it's cold out there today its cold out there
then put your little hand in mine there ain't no hill or mountain we can't climb babe I got
you babe I got you babe ok campers rise and shine and don't forget your booties because
it's cold out there today its cold out
then put your little hand in mine there ain't no hill or mountain we can't climb babe I got
you babe I got you babe ok campers rise and shine and don't forget your booties because
it's cold out there today its cold
then put your little hand in mine there ain't no hill or mountain we can't climb babe I got
you babe I got you babe ok campers rise and shine and don't forget your booties because
it's cold out there today its
then put your little hand in mine there ain't no hill or mountain we can't climb babe I got
you babe I got you babe ok campers rise and shine and don't forget your booties because
it's cold out there today
then put your little hand in mine there ain't no hill or mountain we can't climb babe I got
you babe I got you babe ok campers rise and shine and don't forget your booties because
it's cold out there
then put your little hand in mine there ain't no hill or mountain we can't climb babe I got
you babe I got you babe ok campers rise and shine and don't forget your booties because
it's cold out
then put your little hand in mine there ain't no hill or mountain we can't climb babe I got
you babe I got you babe ok campers rise and shine and don't forget your booties because
it's cold

then put your little hand in mine there ain't no hill or mountain we can't climb babe I got you babe I got you babe ok campers rise and shine and don't forget your booties because it's
then put your little hand in mine there ain't no hill or mountain we can't climb babe I got you babe I got you babe ok campers rise and shine and don't forget your booties because
then put your little hand in mine there ain't no hill or mountain we can't climb babe I got you babe I got you babe ok campers rise and shine and don't forget your booties
then put your little hand in mine there ain't no hill or mountain we can't climb babe I got you babe I got you babe ok campers rise and shine and don't forget your
then put your little hand in mine there ain't no hill or mountain we can't climb babe I got you babe I got you babe ok campers rise and shine and don't forget
then put your little hand in mine there ain't no hill or mountain we can't climb babe I got you babe I got you babe ok campers rise and shine and don't
then put your little hand in mine there ain't no hill or mountain we can't climb babe I got you babe I got you babe ok campers rise and shine and
then put your little hand in mine there ain't no hill or mountain we can't climb babe I got you babe I got you babe ok campers rise and shine
then put your little hand in mine there ain't no hill or mountain we can't climb babe I got you babe I got you babe ok campers rise and
then put your little hand in mine there ain't no hill or mountain we can't climb babe I got you babe I got you babe ok campers rise
then put your little hand in mine there ain't no hill or mountain we can't climb babe I got you babe I got you babe ok campers
then put your little hand in mine there ain't no hill or mountain we can't climb babe I got you babe I got you babe ok
then put your little hand in mine there ain't no hill or mountain we can't climb babe I got you babe I got you babe
then put your little hand in mine there ain't no hill or mountain we can't climb babe I got you babe I got you
then put your little hand in mine there ain't no hill or mountain we can't climb babe I got you babe I got
then put your little hand in mine there ain't no hill or mountain we can't climb babe I got you babe I
then put your little hand in mine there ain't no hill or mountain we can't climb babe I got you babe
then put your little hand in mine there ain't no hill or mountain we can't climb babe I got you
then put your little hand in mine there ain't no hill or mountain we can't climb babe I got
then put your little hand in mine there ain't no hill or mountain we can't climb babe I
then put your little hand in mine there ain't no hill or mountain we can't climb babe
then put your little hand in mine there ain't no hill or mountain we can't climb
then put your little hand in mine there ain't no hill or mountain we can't
then put your little hand in mine there ain't no hill or mountain we
then put your little hand in mine there ain't no hill or mountain

then put your little hand in mine there ain't no hill or
then put your little hand in mine there ain't no hill
then put your little hand in mine there ain't no
then put your little hand in mine there ain't
then put your little hand in mine there

then put your little hand in mine
then put your little hand in
then put your little hand
then put your little
then put your
then put
then

RELEASE: 7 May 1993
DIRECTOR: Harold Ramis

In the Company of Men

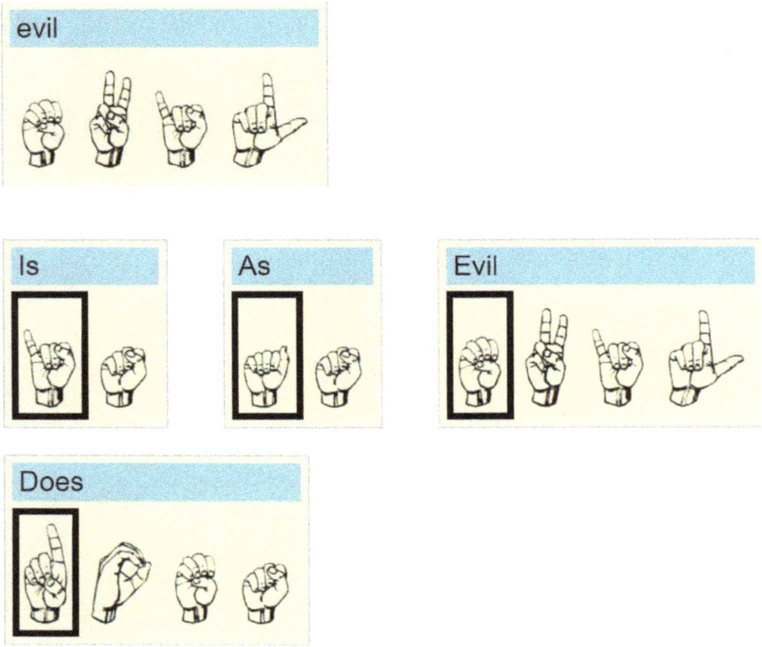
evil
Is
As
Evil
Does

RELEASE: 1 August 1997
DIRECTOR: Neil Labute

SPUTNIK

I AM DENNIS LEBEDEV
I FIX CARS
I CHAT ONLINE WITH MY FRIEND MASHA
HER EGGS ARE THE INSECT UNIVERSE.
I WATCH STEAM FILMS.

I AM THE AGREEMENT MONSTER.

AS I WAS SAYING
I AGREE WITH TANYA
THE ORPHANAGE
IS THE SPACE

THE HOST AND THE PARASITE
THE ALIEN IN THE BODY
THE DéCOR OF THE PAST

SEMIRADOV IS THE WORD OF AN OFFICER
YEA YEA WE ALL RETURNED TO EARTH
WITHDANGEROUS ORGANISM LIVING
INSIDE US.

DENNIS HE A CREATURE LIVING
IN THE ESOPHAGUS
OF A COSMONAUT.

HE EATS CRIMINAL.

RELEASE: 14 August 2020
DIRECTOR: Egor Abramenko

Falling Down

Not pushing or tripping but falling
suggesting being up before being downed
like the formal dormant indignation
that readily becomes moral murderousness
bipping knowing satire into justifying
the nice hot cod that swims in the heat
of most americans
like the snap of excuse
the not-fault of another / accident
and just not knowing because it is the cosmos
combining againsting
godding causing funded or founded for a falling.

RELEASE: 26 February 1993
DIRECTOR: Joel Schumacher

A Zed and Two Noughts

o alright, phone for an ambulance, I've had enough *

suit yourself / look after yourself *

etiquette was never your strong suit *

I'm bleeding. you always come when I'm bleeding

there are only 23 letters in the greek alphabet

legless prostitute of marseilles, buried in a full coffin with steel legs made for another man

the body rots, the legs remain

m is for monkey

m is for mercury poisoning / maybe keep prawns to recreate the smell

may I ask you a question in advancement of this child's education?

grief doesn't taste like anything sour.

in a zoo community there are deaths everyday. crocodiles are not important

venus and the unicorn, nun, [illegible]

so I'm to be a kept woman?

NOT SO YOU'D NOTICE

Can I have a word?

clipped wings

is leglessness a form of contra conception? a pregnant cripple

Teddy bear's picnic

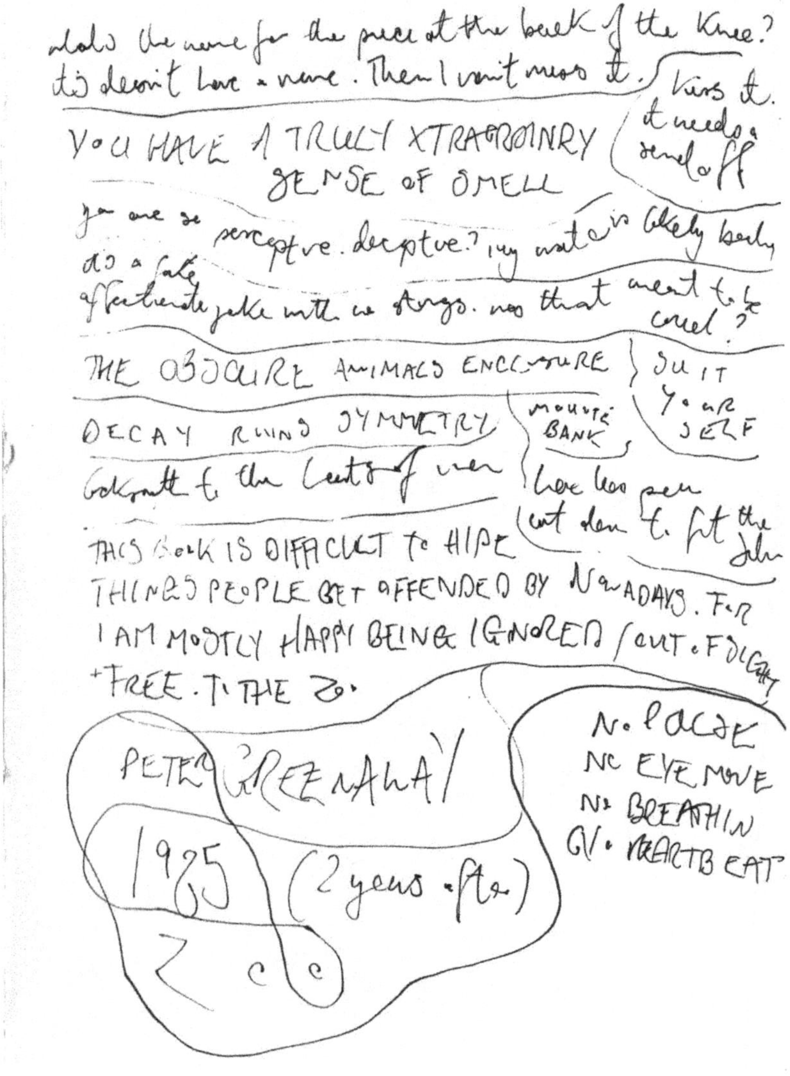
whats the name for the piece at the back of the knee?
it doesn't have a name. Then I can't miss it.
Kiss it. it needs a send off
YOU HAVE A TRULY XTRAORDINRY SENSE OF SMELL
you are so perceptive. deceptive? my watch is likely badly
as a fate
affectionate joke with no stings. was that meant to be cruel?
THE OBSCURE ANIMALS ENCLOSURE
SUIT YOUR SELF
DECAY RUINS SYMMETRY
MOUNTE BANK
Godspeed to the hearts of men
have been seen cut down to fit the film
THIS BOOK IS DIFFICULT TO HIDE
THINGS PEOPLE GET OFFENDED BY NOWADAYS. FOR
I AM MOSTLY HAPPY BEING IGNORED / OUT OF DELICACY
+FREE TO THE ZOO
NO PACE
NO EYE MOVE
NO BREATHIN
GV. HEARTBEAT
PETER GREENAWAY
1985 (2 years after)
ZOO

RELEASE: 4 October 1985
DIRECTOR: Peter Greenaway

The Falls

A strange way to not do what ever habit
is not knowable to people who don't use what they have
but bin it and run the taps to make sound
as if a group of working, exercising, active limbs
is good when not used but left in the chamber, or tank,
if you wish to fish to the animal list
and whether that list, those people,
that family square of adaptation
that uses you to find fire to light,
to make impersonations of birds,
before the unknown violent event
during the play called little green finches
performed for a film called the reluctant singer
with random fluttering gestures
is the habit of singing through an almost closed mouth.

Whether it chew days off, is the indecipherable question,
whether it rests or something else that isn't a miserable
brief smoke cloud that moves in the weather
that learns finally to properly swing and squat and clean and jerk
until the cables come loose and its a brief respite in the skies
like trains cutting Pollie's (my favourite) language, Mickel-ease
and twelve another's you didn't see
just as she speaks no other of the new post-VUE tongues
not a word of Abcadefghan, Agalese, Agreet, Allow, Allow-ease
Althuese, Antoneen, Betelguese, Candoese, Capistan
Carn-est-aero, Cathaganian, Cathanay, Curdine, Entree
Fallaver, Foreignester, Glendower, Glozel, Hapaxlegomena
Hartileas B., Instantaneious Dekis, Ipostan, Itino Re
Karnash, Kantan, Katan, Kath-a-ganian, Maudine
O-Lev-Lit, Os-leet-ter, Orthocathalian, Regest
Sackamayer, U-thalian, Untowards, nor bloody Vionester

Languages are all an animal name group we lean on
like lamby and chimpy talk, and the summaries of our natural ways

like Pollie, who asks, in Mickel-ese, pronounced in high registers,
why waiting for the next syllable is like waiting for a child
to scream, after it has fallen? why not before?
She sings whether habitat is connected to habit
like clothing you smell? Or whether diamond
is a rough word for fruit? Or for whatever you associate
with conversation? It is a delaying tactic,
and yet it is whether you know it or not.

Film is a body that puts things inside of people,
which asks whether you wrote that
because its too good for you to have done so
and leads the author to think whether they did
out of habit, theft, asking whether habit is theft,
or conditioning, or soul, or whatever you want.
it's just a list of delaying tactics that are better than say a pinch
whether a hand is placed on a throat or chest
chin or chest, or picked up, it comes to mind.
two hands wrapped around neck, whether the neck
of a fish, bird or person, or a skull base, it's a height
whether you notice or not. it's your mouth cupped
around a hole that's just beneath a skin.
whether you pull the skeleton from the body, or not
its a plum. a chin, chest, shoulder blades, wings
a damage, to hold, to offer an intermediary delay
between conversation, whether you swim hands in
or fold elbows, whether its music or not or a suggestion.
it's then a pick up, a cutting of walking words in the film of habit
it makes two small holes in all the rubbish around you
in your habits, because it's different now
after the violent unknown event, so you might as well
stay on it, daily, repeating, confused, like the Mickel-ese
which stretches the voice box of humans
to influence the very language of animals
and goes back to also doing human imitations, like that were easy.

RELEASE: 1980
DIRECTOR: Peter Greenaway

Prospero's Books

THE Book of
WATER

RELEASE: 25 October 1991
DIRECTOR: Peter Greenaway

The Greenaway Alphabet

Aleph was an ox, a premier sign because it represents strength, the elemental energy that sets everything into motion which changes being to existence, while B was the name of someone missing. A promise to take one's life before the age of eighty. Meanwhile, C was gimmel the camel, that which holds water and allows travel. The animal vehicle that carries one into the beyond. A nice square frame. D was the name of feeling something is missing. That something definitely not human, while E was Heh, the human at prayer, and breath itself. Two arms outward. An ironic turn from realistic to unconvincingly optimistic. G was Zayin, the letter G is the letter Z, a confrontation or face to face encounter. Zayin means weapon in Hebrew, after all. I was yod, with J and Y, and is a hand. A hand offering, but not a handshake. By no means. K was Kaf, the palm of the hand, upfaced and preparing, endlessly. Hitting and missing with equal measure as L was the forgetting to forget something, or someone. But that not being the tradition of which one chooses to be within. M was Mem, was water, stream, waves, movement, dynamism, current. It is questioning of movement, while N was the fleeting urge to apologise. O was Ayin, is the eye, the circle used to be not round, fat and bulged. The orb, ring, around circle, while P, conveniently, was the delivery from remembering. Q was the letter Qof, ape. It was quoff, cut, slice, split, blade, a separate flow. S was the letter shin, tooth, grinding, crushing, breaking assimilating the external into the internal, while U was vav, same root as F, folk and volk as W was same as u, Vav, upside down water. The missing Other letters were like notes, forgotten because of focus on the present project. They were less mysterious and more pointless, unless wielded into a upcoming system, like a memory of a pristine symbolic justified snobbery.

RELEASE: 21 November 2017
DIRECTOR: Saskia Boddeke

Drowning by Numbers

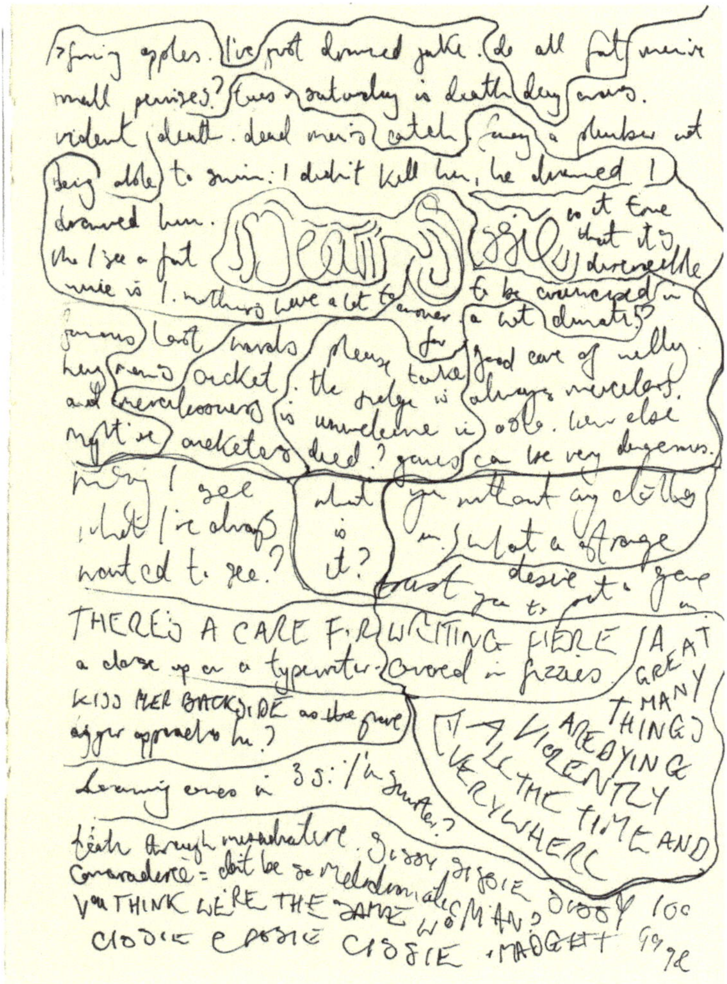
THERE'S A CARE FOR WRITING HERE
KISS HER BACKSIDE as the grave digger approaches her?
A GREAT MANY THINGS ARE DYING VIOLENTLY ALL THE TIME AND EVERYWHERE
YOU THINK WE'RE THE SAME WOMAN

RELEASE: 5 October 1988
DIRECTOR: Peter Greenaway

Homeward Bound : The Incredible Journey

with Julia Rose Lewis

No single criticism for a golden shadow.
Obviously, that is the name for a black lab.
A homeward obit.
The inner voice dog brain is such a sieve.
It's mean tending to destiny and hazard defined,
all the live fish inside are kept alive.
The dog brain only out of water for seconds.

We are bound to remember chance.
Chance was known as an animal right and vegetarian.
Ben, Rattler, and Tiki were portraying Shadow, Chance, and Sassy,
who receive star billing in the film, but, in reality,
Chance and Shadow were each played by four dogs
while Sassy was played by just shy
a century worth of cats.

RELEASE: 3 February 1993
DIRECTOR: Duwayne Dunham

The Thing

RELEASE: 25 June 1982
DIRECTOR: John Carpenter

Alice Doesn't Live Here Anymore

to think ill of m**A**nkind
and not wish i**L**l upon men
Is the highest wisdom
when the most **C**owardly
ar**E** the most vengeful

a boy of no small **D**ignity
does n**O**t love
th**E**ory
a**S** wisdom
instead the most e**N**vious
of o**T**hers seek his mothers

coward**L**y are those men
who th**I**nk ill of Alice
who forgi**V**es
those who ar**E**

t**H**e
most d**E**vious
of fathe**R**s clothed as
th**E**

we**A**k
a**N**d
witt**Y** few who
Muscle
t**O**rtuous lengths of love
that proves her ad**R**esslessness leaps
l**E**ft without man

RELEASE: 9 December 1974
DIRECTOR: Martin Scorsese

Jurassic Park

The early 1990s are Alan Grant pretending to be electrocuted to amuse small children. Tim and Lex, who have been through significant trauma, enjoy the joke and quickly forget. Everything in perspective. Dennis Nedry's death is horrible, for example, and the lawyer dies because he is immoral. Yet the game keeper, who agrees to die, was my favourite memory. I queue'd in front of the Newquay Camelot. The sea was behind the cinema. Why does the raptor pause for dramatic effect, I wondered? How does Alan Grant sing brontosaurus? And how clever can the raptor be that clever if it runs into it's own reflection?

RELEASE: 16 July 1993
DIRECTOR: Steven Spielberg

The Lost World

a world where the thought of a dino sleeps inside
where were it not for the catastrophe that befell them
they would've been the dominant birdbabies

not so much lost as everywhere
the dinosaurs who fruit split people
who are bound to spill human fruit
who have delivered dinner most every night

o but here is roland tembo, a boola on isla nublar
all after having our site b somewhere ...
aware of big game and elephant gunning

he spies a full t-rex so loud on its portable telephone
and its bringing him chocolate as an angry couple
okay but his job is to remember human beef is not nice

like mosquitoes there roland is so strong
carrying dengue and zika, biting that terrible lizard
so tired after being so 'hyper'

the trex is eating people, irritated, degenerate,
synthetic in time of dying so round the corner
like it was yesterday's extinction memories
like whys it getting dark at midday?

a nearby funny diplodocus says
do not drink from the river of deoxyribonucleic acid
it seems trapped on this island!

roland is a death called ness in greater need than most
ashamed, bankrupt, passing my books
around their cave at night to teach dinos to read

good luck! its like rehab in abandoned seaside towns
with extinct visitors in perpetual rain for roland
there is a scent of the looted attraction in those grottos

it is that of prison, or Zoo full of a terrible velociraptor
who asks why clever roland? why seahorses? why are we real?
are we the velicopartor truly a creature of fantasy?

it so clever, it does his thinking for him, packing
roland is a sun in his new heavy black feathers
with a smile like a lover and a giant thick barrel

roland watches a miffed stegosaurus
as an armoured scaler catching its tail on a nail
becoming a stone statue of a sudden Buddha

roland watches a triceratops go truly ganesha
Rolando risks his journey to isla sorna
and begins to understand friendship

which turns out not be so Roland leaves
for blessed are all's god's self portraits,
even those long chosen for deselection

RELEASE: 18 July 1997
DIRECTOR: Steven Spielberg

Jurassic Park 3

ALAN

RELEASE: 20 July 2001
DIRECTOR: Joe Johnston

Lunacy

RELEASE : 17 November 2005
DIRECTOR: Jan Švankmajer

Barton Fink

LOOK UPON ME! LOOK UPON ME! I'LL
SHOW YOU THE LIFE OF THE MIND!!

The fire starts racing down the hallway.
Fire races along the wall-sweat goopus.

LOOK UPON ME! I'LL SHOW YOU THE LIFE
OF THE MIND! I'LL SHOW YOU THE LIFE
OF THE MIND!

...Brother, is it hot.
...Don't look at me like that,
neighbor. It's just me – Charlie.
Jesus, people can be cruel...
...if it's not my build, it's my
personality.
...They say I'm a madman, Barton,
but I'm not mad at anyone. Honest
I'm not. Most guys I just feel sorry
for. Yeah. It tears me up inside, to
think about what they're going
through. How trapped they are. I
understand it. I feel for them. So I
try and help them out...
...Jesus. Yeah. I know what it feels
like, when things get all balled up
at the head office. It puts you
through hell, Barton. So I help people
out. I just wish someone would do as
much for me...
...Jesus it's hot. Sometimes it gets
so hot, I want to crawl right out of
my skin.
Because you DON'T LISTEN!
...Jesus, I'm dripping again.
...C'mon Barton, you think you know

about pain? You think I made your
life hell? Take a look around this
dump. You're just a tourist with a
typewriter, Barton. I live here.
Don't you understand that...
...And you come into MY home... And
you complain that I'M making too...
much... noise.

...I'm sorry.

Don't be.
I'm getting off the merry-go-round.
...I'll be next door if you need me.
...Oh, I dropped in on your folks.
And Uncle Dave?
...Good people. By the way, that
package I gave you? I lied. It isn't
mine.

A horrible moaning sound – almost human – can be heard under the roar of the fire.

RELEASE: 1 January 1991
DIRECTOR: The Coen Brothers

Teen Wolf

with Julia Rose Lewis

Ask nebraska if you're allowed, if forever means forever
if a hardware store run by werewolves, needs to sell whistles?
If an explanation is really long overdue?

Ob
conscious: the movie is the film of fun for itself?
If fever is as fever reads the founding of rome,
wolf cubs back to the future, milk and jeans.

If a panelvan can become a surfboard and a town road an ocean,
then a werewolf can do a handstand to demand attention.

The wolf wanders between the girl needing attention and the girl paying
him
attention as a given thing also known as urban surfing.
I remember saying life sucks *then you die* to the mirror.

If and only if a basketball will fall into the net
it's a better bet for testosterone, for the girl practicing with her
dadwolf?

For her, the tomatoes rippened, as the wolf is himself a peach.
Wolf in the nightshade family. Those famished chats.

RELEASE: 23 August 1985
DIRECTOR: Rod Daniel

Come and See

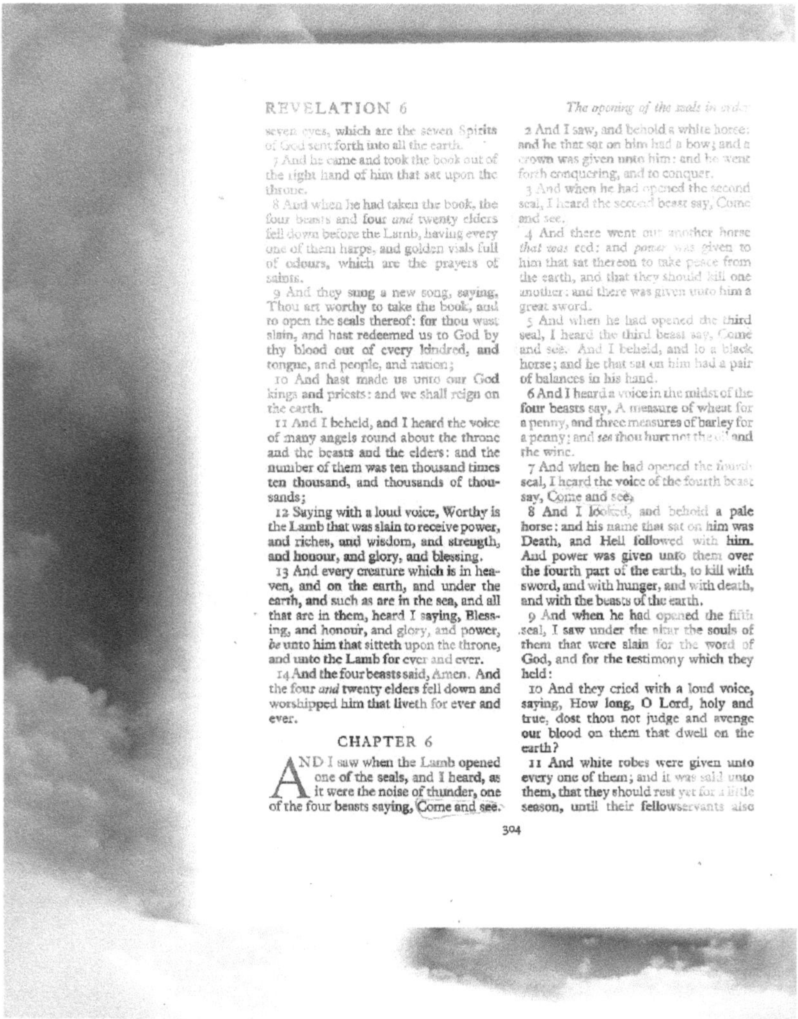
REVELATION 6 — *The opening of the seals in order*

seven eyes, which are the seven Spirits
of God sent forth into all the earth.
7 And he came and took the book out of
the right hand of him that sat upon the
throne.
8 And when he had taken the book, the
four beasts and four *and* twenty elders
fell down before the Lamb, having every
one of them harps, and golden vials full
of odours, which are the prayers of
saints.
9 And they sung a new song, saying,
Thou art worthy to take the book, and
to open the seals thereof: for thou wast
slain, and hast redeemed us to God by
thy blood out of every kindred, and
tongue, and people, and nation;
10 And hast made us unto our God
kings and priests: and we shall reign on
the earth.
11 And I beheld, and I heard the voice
of many angels round about the throne
and the beasts and the elders: and the
number of them was ten thousand times
ten thousand, and thousands of thou-
sands;
12 Saying with a loud voice, Worthy is
the Lamb that was slain to receive power,
and riches, and wisdom, and strength,
and honour, and glory, and blessing.
13 And every creature which is in hea-
ven, and on the earth, and under the
earth, and such as are in the sea, and all
that are in them, heard I saying, Bless-
ing, and honour, and glory, and power,
be unto him that sitteth upon the throne,
and unto the Lamb for ever and ever.
14 And the four beasts said, Amen. And
the four *and* twenty elders fell down and
worshipped him that liveth for ever and
ever.

CHAPTER 6

AND I saw when the Lamb opened
one of the seals, and I heard, as
it were the noise of thunder, one
of the four beasts saying, Come and see.
2 And I saw, and behold a white horse:
and he that sat on him had a bow; and a
crown was given unto him: and he went
forth conquering, and to conquer.
3 And when he had opened the second
seal, I heard the second beast say, Come
and see.
4 And there went out another horse
that was red: and *power* was given to
him that sat thereon to take peace from
the earth, and that they should kill one
another: and there was given unto him a
great sword.
5 And when he had opened the third
seal, I heard the third beast say, Come
and see. And I beheld, and lo a black
horse; and he that sat on him had a pair
of balances in his hand.
6 And I heard a voice in the midst of the
four beasts say, A measure of wheat for
a penny, and three measures of barley for
a penny; and *see* thou hurt not the oil and
the wine.
7 And when he had opened the fourth
seal, I heard the voice of the fourth beast
say, Come and see.
8 And I looked, and behold a pale
horse: and his name that sat on him was
Death, and Hell followed with him.
And power was given unto them over
the fourth part of the earth, to kill with
sword, and with hunger, and with death,
and with the beasts of the earth.
9 And when he had opened the fifth
seal, I saw under the altar the souls of
them that were slain for the word of
God, and for the testimony which they
held:
10 And they cried with a loud voice,
saying, How long, O Lord, holy and
true, dost thou not judge and avenge
our blood on them that dwell on the
earth?
11 And white robes were given unto
every one of them; and it was said unto
them, that they should rest yet for a little
season, until their fellowservants also

304

RELEASE: 1985
DIRECTOR: E. Klimov

Black Robe

Whomever rejects their demons badgers us to death with angels.
Henri Michaux

Where talking cannot travel
Where what is known leaves behind
Where torture's line
Where preaching floors
Where repeating frontiers
Where bravery is relation
Where small is born continually
Where it soon became clear (in spiritual adolescence)
I had been born to live among monsters

Where the eye were round and self-contained
Where through the lids night would enter in
Where the bestial comes from out from shadows
Where sleep and hair must bestride my lord
Where in all loops and turns our feet devour the dust
Father whispers it has soon become clear (from adolescence on)
that I had been born to lie amongst men.

RELEASE: 5 September 1991
DIRECTOR: Bruce Beresford

Heat

The claim of Neil McCauley's obsessive purpose as theft. The pretence that Vincent Hanna's is McCauley himself. Around the gunfights; principles of professionalism, forbearance, commitment, research and sacrifice. The inability to be two things at once.

What people embody, like layers, with this being the middlemost. The uppermost suggests the guns are like toys.

The internet movie firearm database provides a kind of poetry. Its author mentions that during the armored car robbery, Chris Shiherlis uses a Colt Model 733 short-barreled carbine as his *weapon of choice.*

The lowermost level, the true core of the film is not dualism. It is the statement *That's not necessary* responded to with the question *Does it have to be necessary?*

The Colt Model 733 are compact versions of the M16 rifle family with 11.5-inch barrels, familiar even to casual viewers. Allegedly, footage of Shiherlis expertly reloading his rifle during the bank robbery shootout has been shown to Special Forces trainees, with the message from their instructor, *"This is how I want you to reload."*

I will not spend my life at work. I am here, instead, choosing the role of Nate. An incarnation, a muttering bunker. A watcher of the living who thrives in the ruins of murdered people.

The lowermost level begins to emerge. If the planet itself is the metaphor, warmth resides in the core. The film can be said to be encapsulated in the phrase *let it go*. Let Waingro go. To live is to learn to let it go. For whatever it is, it isn't worth returning to.

⊠According to the on-set armorer, Hanna's rifle was a Select Fire FNC-80 assault rifle that was chopped down by the armorer to a Para length barrel, and an M16 style birdcage was attached.

Easy to say, hard to know. Experience over knowledge. The act of borrowing trouble as a way to learning. Being interested in the bank's money, not ours.

Michael Mann is insisting on the realistic echo of guns.

Despite being a full auto weapon, Mann instructed Pacino to fire only in semi-automatic mode. Hanna and the cops in the shootout would be concerned about the possibility of endangering bystanders.

Eyes hold little expression, contrary to popular opinion. Neil McCauley was a real person.

Do not make your loved ones wait at such a pivotal time in the relationship. Hanna shoots a man holding a child. They are nearly just too old.

During the armoured car robbery, Michael Cheritto uses a 20" barreled FN FAL 50.61 Paratrooper version with a side-folding stock. He executes the third guard with a double tap to the sternum and a third shot to the head.

This is a military tactic known as a Failure Drill or Mozambique Drill, and is a prominent feature in Michael Mann's films.

Charlene chops her hand to the right. It is a symbol that someone is here, and to run, while Lauren is limp in Vincent's arms with femoral bleed. The grim reaper is visiting upon you, says Waingro.

Vincent Hanna asks, knowing the answer, *What are they looking at?* Neil McCauley, asks,*What am I doing?* and answers his own question. *I'm talking to a blank telephone, cause there is a dead man on the other end of this fucking line...*

The Failure Drill appears twice in Heat - the incident above, and then at the end, when McCauley executes Waingro in his hotel room.

Neil and Vincent hold hands. At the lowermost level, Neil has turned back for Eady. To let one you love out
of your life
by dying.

RELEASE: 12 June 1997
DIRECTOR: Michael Mann

The Dunwich Horror

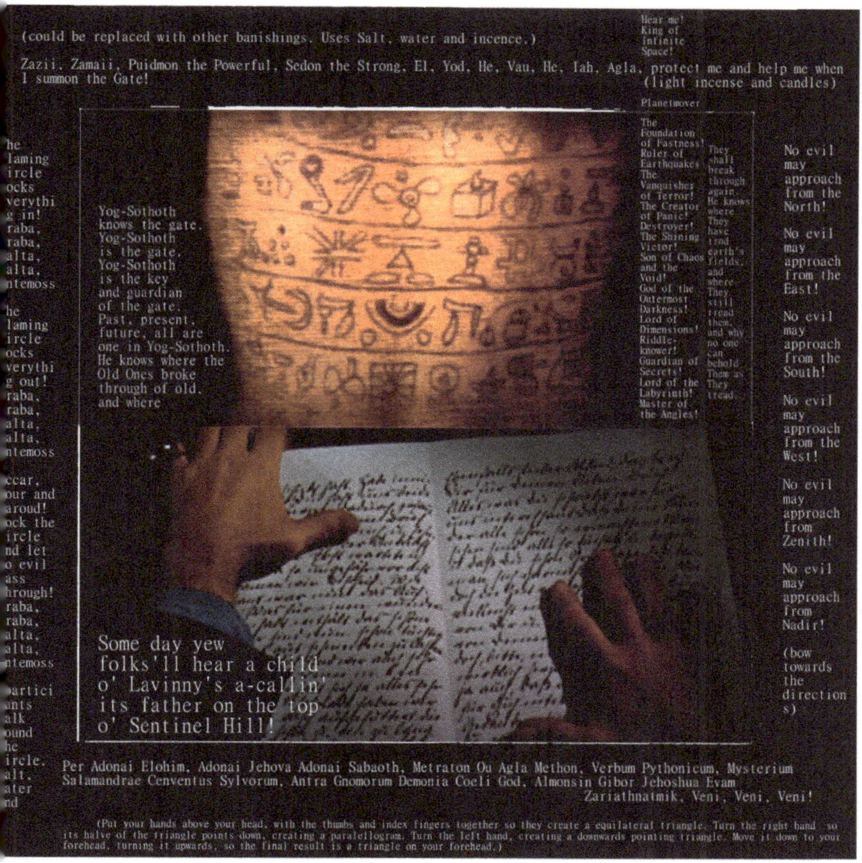

Hear me! King of Infinite Space!
(could be replaced with other banishings. Uses Salt, water and incence.)
Zazii, Zamaii, Puidmon the Powerful, Sedon the Strong, El, Yod, He, Vau, He, Iah, Agla, protect me and help me when I summon the Gate!
(light incense and candles)
Planetmover
The Foundation of Fastness! Ruler of Earthquakes The Vanquisher of Terror! The Creator of Panic! Destroyer! The Shining Victor! Son of Chaos and the Void! God of the Outermost Darkness! Lord of Dimensions! Riddle-knower! Guardian of Secrets! Lord of the Labyrinth! Master of the Angles!
They shall break through again. He knows where They have trod earth's fields, and where They still tread them, and why no one can behold Them as They tread.
Yog-Sothoth knows the gate. Yog-Sothoth is the gate. Yog-Sothoth is the key and guardian of the gate. Past, present, future, all are one in Yog-Sothoth. He knows where the Old Ones broke through of old, and where
No evil may approach from the North!
No evil may approach from the East!
No evil may approach from the South!
No evil may approach from the West!
No evil may approach from Zenith!
No evil may approach from Nadir!
(bow towards the directions)
Some day yew folks'll hear a child o' Lavinny's a-callin' its father on the top o' Sentinel Hill!
Per Adonai Elohim, Adonai Jehova Adonai Sabaoth, Metraton Ou Agla Methon, Verbum Pythonicum, Mysterium Salamandrae Cenventus Sylvorum, Antra Gnomorum Demonia Coeli God, Almonsin Gibor Jehoshua Evam Zariathnatmik, Veni, Veni, Veni!
(Put your hands above your head, with the thumbs and index fingers together so they create a equilateral triangle. Turn the right hand so its halve of the triangle points down, creating a paralellogram. Turn the left hand, creating a downwards pointing triangle. Move it down to your forehead, turning it upwards, so the final result is a triangle on your forehead.)

RELEASE: 14 January 1970
DIRECTOR: Daniel Haller

Peter Pan

with Prudence Bussey-Chamberlain

to have a fat and irate father
in a room with the nursemaid
dog pouring tonic into spoons
and licking paws medicinal properties
pan pirate poppycock
it all starts in the stories
we get too old for
where the hook is on
your left hand not right
now George now George
sent to a room of his own
where the nursery & the puppy
stop at nothing but building blocks
and errant skates and children are
kidnapped when the window is left open
so call the police and see how well
they never never land
to be a lost boy is so
poet to brawl and fight
fashion weapons out of supermarket
chain go underground
& mystical appropriation where
the substance nights are long
heavy lit up moments
to be a beat
is so lost and violent shanking
in the jungle where here bottle tops
smashed necks a jugular in leaf-green
dress
mismatch rhythm of clothes
mob mentality and gangs that war
eye-patched and one-handed
you carry your markings forever
which are only a trauma in ink
you can tell us stories
and we will call you Mother

you cannot be lost or beat or boy
women tell their stories with their
ovaries; they must; they need to
n the experimental fairy
nightmares syncopate to dawn
green reverse tulip dresses
Tinkerbelle of trouble
beauty, where in the affective
light of an emotional disco
I was in love with Tigerlily
this whole time
one day, a lantern, ablaze with
reconciliation under the bell
jar turned red glow with anger & trying
in opportunity for flight like jet
or standing in your window
posed, hands on hips, and legs a step apart
the bell-ringing heroes are always
a Judas and pendulous flower-like
move towards their fates, resigned.
with your dangerous metal hand &
your distant look
            pirational and a crocodile
on your shoulder; here is the tick of a
time-bombing around the landscape
so old beat so faux
looking all bourgeoisie with that
plumey hat and knee high boots
when the ship is air authority
tight with planks and yoga
downward dog the right hand man
to time's rising sun.
the cabin boy is the one true fairy
in a world of wings
until you believe
until you clap
until you say it aloud
all of us will be dying

RELEASE: 27 July 1953
DIRECTORS: Hamilton Luske, Wilfred Jackson, Clyde Geronimi

Colour Out of Space

Don't say sorry to me.

RELEASE: 7 September 2019
DIRECTOR: Richard Stanley

Alien

the facehugger ejaculates alien eggs ()()()()()()()()()
down the throats {of people}

the alien babies ⊠ grow into the stomach >>>>>>>
>>>>>>> like a wom

Ridley brings with him / ⊠ the psychoanalytical
⊠ subtlety of Hartlepool

the Alien is deathu, deathish, a bored lick %

it's a * John Hurt ⊠ holding a cockerel ⊠
Sigourney Weaver chewing = a monster.
Ian Holm a ⊠ fan of the coiled + snake.
Giger is in the back with his stairs *

at least the / crew \ look like real people

the xenomorph ||| is a wet seated ape, a yawning | purring | sleeping
| cat of punishment

WELL THERE'S YOUR
PROBLEM

RELEASE: 6 September 1979
DIRECTOR: Ridley Scott

Aliens

the moist intimidating < plural > of all times
the most panicky) marine (of hope
the most best newt {us} surviving the night
by hide and seek champion

why not send synthetic >> to fight the alien?
<war is worse / \ but undeniably curious
⍰but this is my face 2020. warless.
just more acid to spull

death, ^*pacifism won't work*^ says Ripley
in space, *this is the highest place of pain,*
for the earth is always awa……y from us.

she thinks, ||| I'd never imagine
an alien drowning |||
that *humans* indulge
themselves
up until the point = they are
no longer allowed to

death is active around their
skin yet Paul Reiser still tries
to take one home etc… ++
while he is seeking its >
weakness ~

a ☒ strong lead
a ☒ rushed planet
to shoot eggs like bitch
more isn't always > better

RELEASE: 29 August 1986
DIRECTOR: James Cameron

Alien[3]

AN
UNFAIR
ADVAN
TAGE

RELEASE: 22 May 1992
DIRECTOR: David Fincher

Alien Resurrection

I know you have a plate so ⊠.
full it is no longer a plate, so }
I'll not be bothersome {{{

it used to be we didn't know where we were.........
it used <<<<<<<<<<<<<<<< life
meaning while >> you were busy
with your splicing << /// ....

birth was incurable as an alien
⍰
the possibilities of all minds
and actions {made hideous babies} ...

you can't control it <<<<<<
<<<you can't ask is it human.
{{{sad......
..........................]]
you won't let that be] still

meaning, it whips out}}}}} a tiny gross
space}}}}} sucks skin}}}}} off

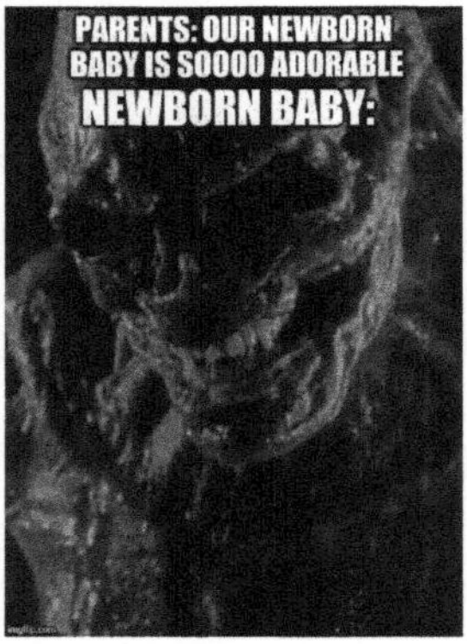
PARENTS: OUR NEWBORN BABY IS SOOOO ADORABLE
NEWBORN BABY:

RELEASE: 6 November 1997
DIRECTOR: Jean-Pierre Jeunet

Alien vs Predator

are we in
the right
film?
when you think about it, it's alien
versus alien really

RELEASE: 22 October 2004
DIRECTOR: Paul WS Anderson

Napoléon

What one wave looks like to another wave.
A camera lashed to a horse, dropped into water.

All red rubber rhyming, and leaking, mute and disappearing
where mensur scars keep on cropping up, cranked by hand.
Victories endlessly to the glory of the French.

They remember his attack was so brilliant. A snowball fight.
The twin figure of a man, falling upon the flaring of imagination,
see Byron's Ode or Stendhal's Vie military.

Too much then the emperor in his meals, dark matter
across Europe, rapid cutting. It is easy to describe
the long work from freedom. Danton giving a speech.

Napoléon wiring up the hammer,
sitting in his room, with the terror outside.

Gance is directing with a revolver, in a fight anyone way,
with handfuls of silent colourlessness, with the dying, screaming,
weeping scaled men on grass. With Cendrars, Kipling,
D'Annunzio, more fit to stand than sit in blue.

Those who flee defeat as a grand gift in the human head
between two fingers in perspective, can always be
put back together later, be they of film or republic.

RELEASE: 1927
DIRECTOR: Abel Gance

Henry : portrait of a serial killer

It’s nasty stuff but it probably happened
though it didn’t
though I shouldn’t have probably watched it at 14
but I’m glad I did learn
the nicknames for nasty stuff
for flat voiced seduction of kicking tvs and then
smashing them over heads
and video-taping what murder might actually
look like rather than the popular killing
films that are very popular.
Not ideal that everyone exists on a spectrum of evil
possibility, but wise enough to depict
how boring is disgusting stomach churning boring
how some see others as not being
and treat them thusly from brain damage and nasty
grainy repulsive gut greys and suitcases full of nasty stuff
Probably best but also not prescriptable

RELEASE: 5 January 1990
DIRECTOR: John McNaughton

The Lighthouse

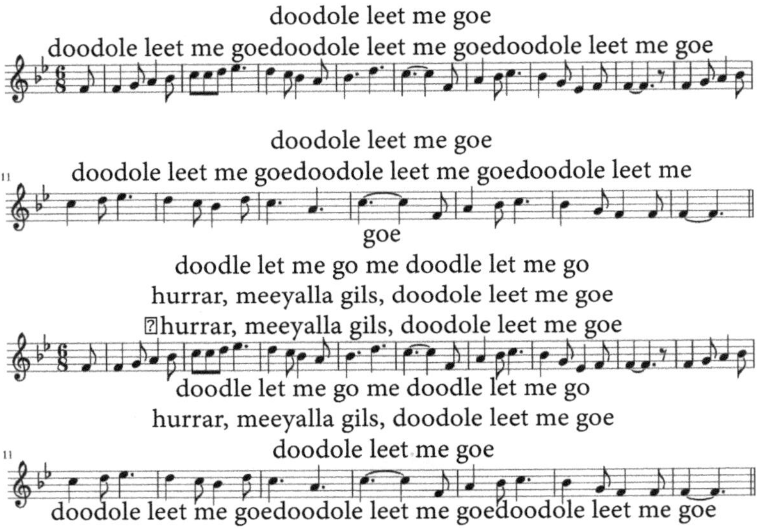
doodole leet me goe
doodole leet me goedoodole leet me goedoodole leet me goe
doodole leet me goe
doodole leet me goedoodole leet me goedoodole leet me
goe
doodle let me go me doodle let me go
hurrar, meeyalla gils, doodole leet me goe
hurrar, meeyalla gils, doodole leet me goe
doodle let me go me doodle let me go
hurrar, meeyalla gils, doodole leet me goe
doodole leet me goe
doodole leet me goedoodole leet me goedoodole leet me goe

To be murmured or moaned or cried to the tune of AL Lloyd's interpretation of the shanty Doodle Let Me Go (Yaller Girls) live at the Top Lock Folk Club, Runcorn, on 5 November 1972

RELEASE: 18 October 2019
DIRECTOR: Robert Eggers

Waterloo

Publish and be damned.
Wellington

Marching in step, more budget than film.
It's even hard not to picture the battle,
and the retrospective emphasis on chance.

Wellington's entrance and dialogue made of quotes.
We were lucky to win, it was a damn nice thing,
the nearest run thing you ever saw...

In conclusion, this fight, Bonaparte died.
I worked beside his mask in a museum,
and this seems now to be encased for every war ever.

An American as Nopolean and a Canadian as Wollingtan.
Yet it's best to cover all at the end, in a close-your-eyes
with-your-own hands sort of soporific Sunday watch.

Peninsula panoramas, drowning in an inch of liquid,
warmed by a wave of sentiment from which it was born.
It is hard to miss blood and guts, and big stacks of the dead.

Both men, N + W, seat themselves with the more generous of their
enemies,
appearing to history, as no mistake; for there has been none.
I have seen their backs before, madam, says Wellington to the
hostess.

RELEASE: 26 October 1970
DIRECTOR: Sergei Bondarchuk

Gummo

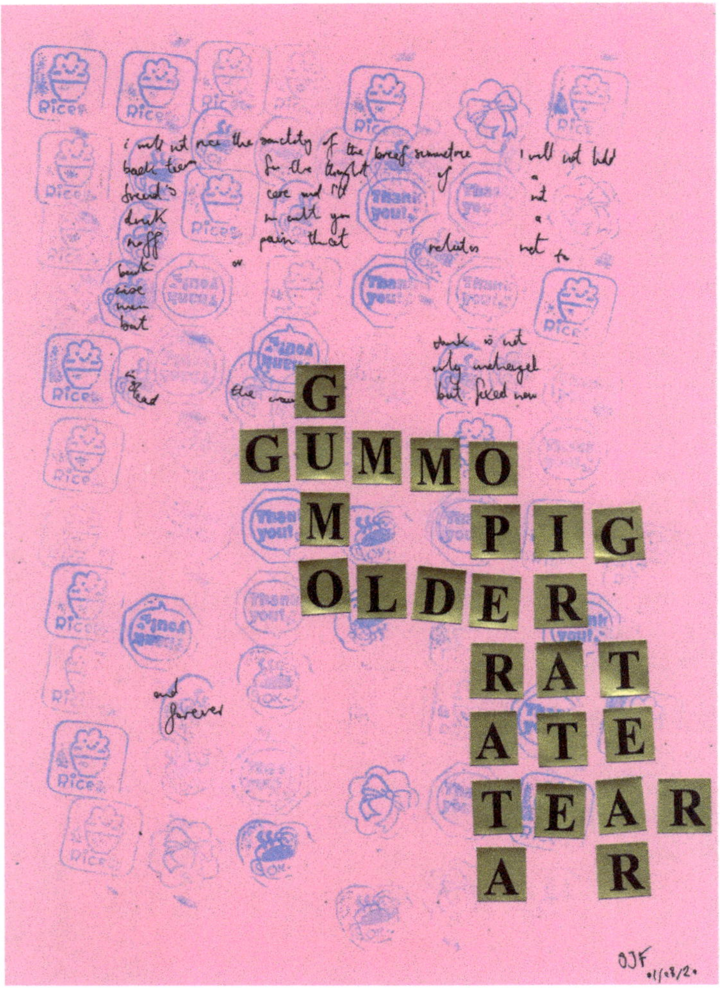
G
GUMMO
M PIG
OLDER R
RAT
ATE
TEAR
A R
OJF

RELEASE: 17 April 1998
DIRECTOR: Harmony Korine

The Frighteners
with Julia Rose Lewis

> all poems are love poems, some poems
> are better off dead
>
> James Galvin

we are what we are spectral lively
and alike wanting to look at the jay
to be tired and serious to be resting anxious face

the jay we came to see grief
means gratuitous forever
this feeling he flees the cemetery
as a spirit flops on sand
the entangled spirit uses the same restraint
techniques I have used
to cover ourselves with a jacket
to control the head shield the teeth

what is it about ghost machetes?
I would manifest a blueberry oyster cult,
a conveniently empty walk in freezer
a pliant act, a mirror obsidian,
a hospital. a figure in a cape. a living from the dead
the sand spirit releasing dopamine through the walls
like fear and reward

is a horror film or a satire of a horrible film
or a mutton bird to whom the third jay is given
it is jays all the way forward
it is Michael also through the wall

RELEASE: 17 July 1996
DIRECTOR: Peter Jackson

(M)(e)(m)(e)(n)(t)(o)

(W)(h)(a)(t) (I) (c)(o)(u)(l)(d)(n)(t) (d)(e)(c)(i)(p)(h)(e)(r)
(d)(e)(s)(p)(i)(t)(e) (t)(h)(e) (r)(e)(v)(e)(l)(a)(t)(i)(o)(n) (o)(f)
(r)(e)(a)(d)(i)(n)(g)

(b)(e)(i)(n)(g) (o)(n)(l)(y) (f)(o)(r) (t)(h)(e) (i)(n)(n)(e)(r) (m)(i)(n)(d)

(i)(s) (h)(o)(w) ?? (f)(o)(r)(g)(e)(t) (e)(v)(e)(r)(y)(t)(h)(i)(n)(g) (I)
(r)(e)(a)(d)

(a) (c)(o)(n)(d)(e)(m)(n)(a)(t)(i)(o)(n) (t)(h)(a)(t) (t)(h)(i)(s)
(s)(t)(r)(u)(c)(k) (s)(o) (h)(a)(r)(d) (I) (b)(e)(g)(a)(n)
(w)(r)(i)(t)(i)(n)(g) (d)(o)(w)(n) (e)(a)(c)(h) (m)(o)(m)(e)(n)(t)

(a)(s) (m)(a)(t)(e)(r)(i)(a)(l) (s)(e)(n)(s)(e)(d)
(u)(n)(i)(d)(e)(n)(t)(i)(f)(i)(e)(d) (i)(n) (t)(h)(e) (w)(o)(r)(d)(s)
(t)(h)(e)(m)(s)(e)(l)(v)(e)(s), (w)(o)(r)(d)(s) (I) (h)(a)(d)
(t)(h)(o)(u)(g)(h)(t) (I)(h)(a)(d) (k)(n)(o)(w)(n), (b)(e)(f)(o)(r)(e)
(t)(h)(e)(y) (w)(e)(r)(e) (a)(r)(r)(a)(n)(g)(e)(d)

(S)(o)(m)(e)(t)(h)(i)(n)(g) (i)(n)(s)(t)(e)(a)(d) (o)(f) (n)(o)(t)(h)(i)(n)(g).

(a) (d)(o)(c)(u)(m)(e)(n)(t)(s)(o) (e)(x)(t)(e)(n)(s)(i)(v)(e) (I)
(b)(e)(g)(i)(n) (t)(o) (c)(o)(n)(c)(e)(i)(v)(e) (o)(f) (t)(h)(e) (i)(d)(e)(a)
(o)(f) (m)(e)(m)(o)(r)(y)

(T)(h)(a)(t) (l)(i)(e)(s) (o)(u)(t)(s)(i)(d)(e) (t)(h)(e) (b)(o)(d)(y)
(t)(h)(a)(t) (h)(o)(l)(d)(s) (t)(h)(e) (b)(r)(a)(i)(n), (l)(i)(k)(e) (a)
(b)(o)(w)(l) (f)(u)(l)(l) (o)(f) (s)(o)(u)(p)

RELEASE: 8 March 2001
DIRECTOR: Christopher Nolan

The Great Outdoors

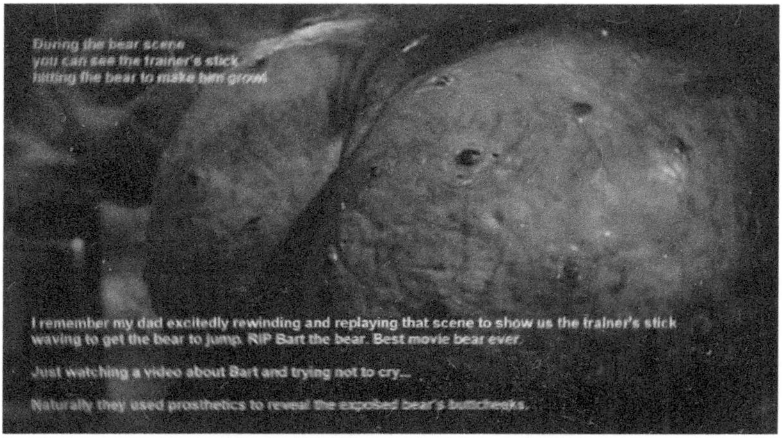
During the bear scene
you can see the trainer's stick
hitting the bear to make him growl
I remember my dad excitedly rewinding and replaying that scene to show us the trainer's stick waving to get the bear to jump. RIP Bart the bear. Best movie bear ever.
Just watching a video about Bart and trying not to cry...
Naturally they used prosthetics to reveal the exposed bear's buttcheeks.

a towering
friend, Bart
in memorial,
far better
than the
humans

RELEASE: 17 June 1988
DIRECTOR: Howard Deutch

Strange Days

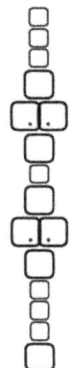

You know how I know it's the end of the world? Everything's already been done. Every kind of music's been tried. Every kind of government's been tried, every hairstyle, bubble gum flavours, you know, breakfast cereal. What are we going to do? How are we going to make another thousand years? I'm telling you, it's over. We used it all up.

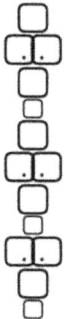

RELEASE: 13 October 1995
DIRECTOR: Kathryn Bigelow

Time of the Wolf

RELEASE: 17 October 2003
DIRECTOR: Michael Haneke

Jacob's Ladder

There exists only the instant present. It is a Now which always and without end is itself new. There is no yesterday nor any tomorrow, but only Now, as it was a thousand years ago and as it will be a thousand years hence.

Meister Eckhart

The price of inaction is far greater than the cost of error.

Meister Eckhart

the sixth rung

almost
I remembered
almost I saw the ladder
for I see it still
eyes closed
picturing it
as I hold it

it is made of twelve steps
and on each step
there are two
human forms

one holds each side
of the step
visible as far as their breasts
clinging

one sees to the top
and there is a face
as of a woman
carved in fire
much more
than terrifying
loving
more than the twenty-four others

for she is over
this central face
though I see the eyes
rarely
crying

the seventh rung

I am definitely in that hour
without climbing
or clutching yet
hands coming for me
to drag me down
to that which
is alone
not gutting
not torture
not sorrow
no purgatory of the cut off
a middle place made by absence
without invasions   humiliations
for there I take in
seeing the smile
as the eyes
cry upon
the ladder
for it is wet
the ladder
as the age
made of chemists
the twelve steps
as periods in which we
take in, by contemplation,
each other
so pours out in
knowing
what is epigraphic
and worth reading

is remembering
and eating

And leaving the earth
resting on lower rungs
I find myself resistable

the eighth rung

I find myself
an altitude
facing down the red
water
trouble
followed
without strength of indifference
like a city
beyond London
I cannot take nor leave

and I climb like dying
feel the rung
that is maybe
release
or division

the devil's are tearing my life away
as I exercise
eat well
abstain
I am sure to die
anyway
sick
refusing
what we are
and were
the opposite
of the end

the ninth rung

this has been
a ladder down
not up for colours for fire
make no difference

this will burn
memories
like chemotherapy of the soul
just chemical
to physical being
on that black ladder
unable to find a day
when I am strong
enough to go
I shall melt into beds
like gulfs
possessed
by readings
familiar with fear our
first time in last moments

familiar with experience
of conversion
too tall for the ladder and to speak of it
saving embarrassment from my friends
whom I no longer recognise
but see as the mangled
whose love I climbed upon
pulling their hair
trapping them
under chairs

to hold their face in my palms
for my submission
into pleasure

for my heartlessness
has hardened into a future

where each hand on the rung
is lifted
to be denied
and laid upon the roof
of a secret house
two lives back

RELEASE: 2 November 1990
DIRECTOR: Adrian Lyne

The Abyss

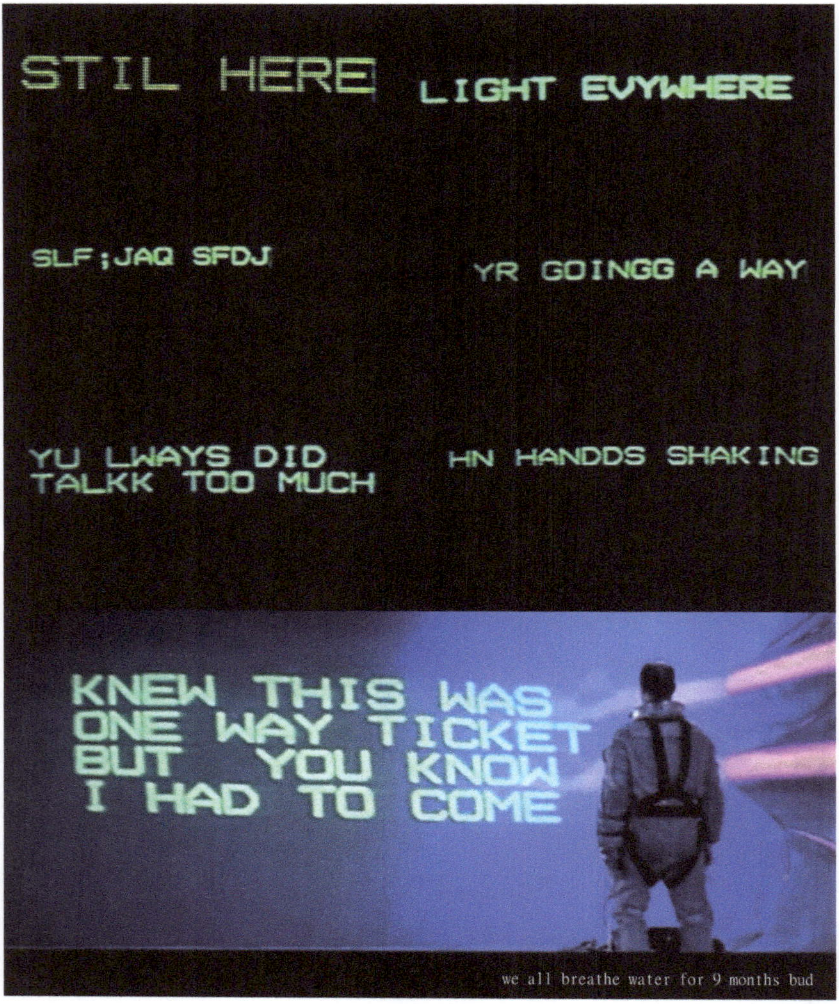
STIL HERE
LIGHT EVYWHERE
SLF;JAQ SFDJ
YR GOINGG A WAY
YU LWAYS DID
TALKK TOO MUCH
HN HANDDS SHAKING
KNEW THIS WAS
ONE WAY TICKET
BUT YOU KNOW
I HAD TO COME
we all breathe water for 9 months bud

RELEASE: 9 August 1989
DIRECTOR: James Cameron

Fata Morgana

RELEASE: 19 April 1971
DIRECTOR: Werner Herzog

A Pigeon Sat on a Branch Reflecting on Existence

o long living life
birds kicking birds
cats calling cats
rats biting rats
the prise money
from deadhands is
a livingsong
a hunter in the snow
a problem of hard conscience
o only so adorable
orignorable as
bones before
their meat fluffing
forever falling
out of beds
and calling it dancing
o what are we doing
when we move?
toward all our troubles
waiting for uncle one tooth
o you cannot feel the day it is
nor forgive
the face paste
despite yourself
I am happy to hear you are thinking fine
writing no one what to be

<i>You have no messages.</i>

- Then the poem ends.
- And then the poem ends?

RELEASE: 24 April 2014
DIRECTOR: Roy Andersson

Acknowledgements

November appeared in the journal Verseville (India) in 2021.

Mishima appeared in the journal Bea Bua (Ireland) in 2021.

Sicario was commissioned for Babelsprech : Eurovision Poetry, in 2018.

Gorillas in the Mist utilises images of Hanabiko "Koko" (1971 - 2018), a pre-eminent Gorilla sign linguist.

Last of Mohicans utilises an image of a black heart, an original artwork by Francis Baker.

Dogtooth, Barton Fink, Margin Call and Gummo appeared in the journal Berfrois (UK) in 2021.

Man Bites Dog appeared in the journal Eurolitkrant (Belgium) in 2021.

Ossuary appeared in the journal of Burning House Press (UK) in 2018.

Irreversible was commissioned by Audiatur Festival (Norway) for their 'Sabotage Seminar' online program and appeared in the film The Swedish Beest, supported by the Embassy of Sweden in the UK, in 2021..

Congo and Alien versus Predator utilise images taken from Photofunia.com

The Vikings appeared in the journal Gorse (Ireland) in 2014 and as part of the Mellom Press (UK) online exhibition Translations in 2020.

The Ghost and the Darkness was commissioned for the anthology The Worked Object : poems in memory of Roy Fisher edited by Peter Robinson et al.

The Burden of Dreams utilises a section of a painting by the artist Monte Dolack, used a film poster in 1983.

Meine Leibste Freunde utilises a section of a poster for La morte ha sorriso all'assassino, 1973, by an unknown artist.

A Zed and Two Noughts and Drowning By Numbers appeared in the book Unfinished Memmoirs of a Hypocrit by SJ Fowler, published by Hesterglock Press (UK) in 2019.

The Falls and Prospero's Books appeared in the journal Hotel (UK) in 2021.

The Greenaway Alphabet was commissioned for the Klangfarbentext project, supported by Lyrik Kabinett and The British Council in 2020.

The Thing and Colour Out of Space are collages made up of separate art-poems drawn from the book I fear my best work behind me by SJ Fowler, published by Stranger Press (UK) in 2017.

The Lost World appeared in the journal Here Comes Everyone (UK) in 2013.

Peter Pan appeared in the book House of Mouse by Prudence Chamberlain Bussey and SJ Fowler, published by Knives Forks and Spoons Press (UK) in 2016.

Alien3 utilises images as a font created by the artist Predaguy.

Napoléon and Waterloo appeared in the journal For Every Year (UK) in 2016.

Time of the Wolf appeared in the Poem Atlas online exhibition 'Refraction' in 2021.

Jacob's Ladder is the second, and final, instalment of a sequence of poems. The first instalment, rungs 1 to 5, were included in the book I will show you the life of the mind (On prescription drugs) by SJ Fowler published by Dostoyevsky Wannabe (UK) in 2020.

On the collaborators:

Maria Malinovskaya was born in Gomel (Belarus) in 1994. She is the author of two books. The first one, a documentary poetry project and collection Kaimaniya (2020), is based on authentic speech of people suffering from mental disorders. The second one, The Movement of Hidden Colonies (2020), includes both lyrical and documentary poems. She lives in Moscow.

Julia Rose Lewis is the author of four poetry collections: High Erratic Ecology, The Hen Wife, Strays, and Phenomenology of the Feral. Her work focuses on incorporating contemporary medical and scientific research into poetry. She remembers the sense of magic she felt watching Michael J. Fox demonstrate the effectiveness of the few available Parkinson's medications on television in 1999.

Prudence Bussey-Chamberlain is a Senior Lecturer in Creative Writing. Her poetry works include Retroviral* (Veer, 2018), Coteries (KFS, 2018) and House of Mouse (KFS, 2017), while she has written critically on contemporary feminism and queer poetics.

FILM YOUR UNREST

www.ingramcontent.com/pod-product-compliance
Lightning Source LLC
Chambersburg PA
CBHW050816090426
42736CB00022B/3477
* 9 7 8 1 9 1 3 6 4 2 3 8 9 *